PUFFIN BOOKS

SUNITA WILLIAMS

Aravinda enjoys writing non-fiction. She has authored another title in the Puffin Lives series, *The 14th Dalai Lama*.

She lives in Bangalore with her family and is rediscovering the world of children's books with her five-year-old son.

Other books in the *Puffin Lives* series

Indira Gandhi: Child of Politics
by Sreelata Menon
Mother Teresa: Apostle of Love
by Rukmini Chawla
Jawaharlal Nehru: The Jewel of India
by Aditi De
Ashoka: The Great and Compassionate King
by Subhadra Sen Gupta
Rani Lakhsmibai: The Valiant Queen of Jhansi
by Deepa Agarwal
Akbar: The Mighty Emperor
by Kavitha Mandana
Mahatma Gandhi: The Father of the Nation
by Subhadra Sen Gupta
The 14th Dalai Lama: Buddha of Compassion
by Aravinda Anantharaman
Swami Vivekananda: A Man with a Vision
by Devika Rangachari
Gautama Buddha: The Lord of Wisdom
by Rohini Chowdhury
Guru Nanak: The Enlightened Master
by Sreelata Menon
Chanakya: The Master of Statecraft
by Deepa Agarwal
B.R.Ambedkar: Saviour of the Masses
by Payal Kapadia

SUNITA WILLIAMS

A STAR IN SPACE

ARAVINDA ANANTHARAMAN

PUFFIN BOOKS
An imprint of Penguin Random House

PUFFIN BOOKS

USA | Canada | UK | Ireland | Australia
New Zealand | India | South Africa | China

Puffin Books is part of the Penguin Random House group of companies whose addresses can be found at global.penguinrandomhouse.com

Published by Penguin Random House India Pvt. Ltd
7th Floor, Infinity Tower C, DLF Cyber City,
Gurgaon 122 002, Haryana, India

Penguin
Random House
India

First published in Puffin by Penguin Books India 2014

Photographs courtesy NASA and the Pandya family

Book design by Tara Upadhyay

10 9 8 7

ISBN 9780143333043

Typeset in Adobe Caslon Pro Eleven Arts, Delhi
Printed at Replika Press Pvt. Ltd, India

www.penguin.co.in

MIX
Paper from responsible sources
FSC www.fsc.org
FSC® C016779

For Gawa,

for an adventure of another kind

Howdy! I'm the Fantastic Fact Ferret!
You'll find me all over this book, furrowing out nuggets of strange and exciting trivia for you.

Contents

Acknowledgements ix

A Childhood Memory 1

- **CHAPTER ONE**
  The Busy Pandya Family 3
- **CHAPTER TWO**
  A Vet in the Making, but Wait, Maybe Not 13
- **CHAPTER THREE**
  'I Can Fly a Copter, Maybe I Can Go to Space' 22
- **CHAPTER FOUR**
  Houston Calling Sunita! 41
- **CHAPTER FIVE**
  Which Way to the International Space Station? 51
- **CHAPTER SIX**
  Meanwhile on Earth . . . 72
- **CHAPTER SEVEN**
  The Home Office 81
- **CHAPTER EIGHT**
  Safe Landings 96

Trivia Treasury 105

Acknowledgements

When I was little and grown-ups asked me what I wanted to be when I grew up, I usually went where my mood took me—shopkeeper, teacher, bookseller . . . it changed often. But for two long years, between the ages of ten and twelve, I'd dreamed of growing up and becoming an astronaut. Next to writing books and becoming a dog doctor, it's the longest ambition I have had.

The telling of this story, of astronaut Sunita Williams, was therefore special since it offered me a view of a world that had fascinated me enormously as a child. What I like about Sunita's story is how so much of it was not planned. She took up whatever came her way with enthusiasm and an openness, and I find that very inspiring. Opportunities presented themselves to her because she was ready for a challenge and so she found herself on the path to space! As career choices go this is totally off the beaten path and she makes it seem like so much fun.

In the writing of this story, there are several people to thank and acknowledge: the Pandya family, especially Dr Deepak Pandya, Mrs Bonnie Pandya and Ms Dina Pandya, and the folks at NASA, Mike Gentry, Gayle Frere and Susan Phipps.

The Internet too proved to be an amazing resource, and I wandered through several websites pausing often as interesting stuff cropped up. But perhaps the one site I read with much interest was Sunita's blog at astrosuni.wordpress.com, which carries her mission logs from both space sojurns. The NASA website itself is packed with information, history, photographs and much more that I returned to it often. I enjoyed too the forums on collectspace.com. Interviews and videos that are available online helped me 'hear' Sunita's voice. I would highly recommend the YouTube video where she takes you on a virtual tour of the ISS! But perhaps what was absolutely special were the two interviews with Sunita Williams herself, where she chatted happily and answered several of my questions.

In the making of this book, I'd like to acknowledge my editors, Sohini Mitra and Mimi Basu, for offering perspective and attention to detail that have made much difference and Nimmy Chacko for going over the proofs with a fine toothcomb. And to my publisher, Penguin Random House, for continuing to support the publication of interesting non-fiction for children.

SUNITA LYN WILLIAMS

BIRTHDAY: 19 September 1965 (51 years old)
PLACE OF BIRTH: Euclid, Ohio

LIVES IN

Houston, Texas or Star City Russia or ISS, Space

FAMILY

Dr Deepak Pandya (father), Ursuline Bonnie Pandya (mother). Michael Williams (husband), Jay Pandya (brother), Dina Pandya (sister), Bailey and Gorby (dogs)

EDUCATION

Needham High School (1983), BS in Physical Sciences, USNA (1987), MS in Engineering Management, Florida Institute of Technology (1995)

CAREER: American Astronaut, US Naval Officer, Flight Instructor, Safety Officer at Naval Test Pilot School

CERTIFICATIONS: Basic Diving Officer (1988), Naval Aviator (1989), Test Pilot (1993)

INTERESTS: Marathons, triathlons, swimming, baseball, snowboarding, bow hunting and windsurfing

HONOURS AND AWARDS: Navy Commendation Medal, Navy and Marine Corps Achievement Medal, Humanitarian Service Medal, Merit in Space Exploration, Padma Bhushan (India), Honorary Doctorate, Gujarat Technological University, Golden Order of Merit (Slovenia) Exploration, Padma Bhushan (India), Honorary Doctorate, Gujarat Technological University, Golden Order of Merit (Slovenia)

FLYING HOURS

Over 3000 hours

MISSION TO SPACE

STS 14 and 15, STS 32 and 33

TIME SPENT IN SPACE: 321 days, seventeen hours and fifteen minutes

SPACEWALKS: Seven totalling fifty hours and forty minutes

SPACE RECORDS: Highest cumulative spacewalk time by a female astronaut, first person to run the Boston Marathon in space

A Childhood Memory

'I want to run too,' Sunita said suddenly.

'Run?' asked her mother.

'The marathon, Mom,' she elaborated, her eyes shining.

'The marathon? The Boston Marathon?'

'Yes!'

Bonnie was taken aback. 'That's over twenty-six miles, Sunita.'

'I know.'

'And you haven't trained for it,' Bonnie continued.

'I know.'

'And it starts in forty-five minutes!' Bonnie said, still reeling at her daughter's sudden plan.

Sunita laughed. 'I know! Will you drive me, Mom? Please?' she asked. She was not yet sixteen and didn't have her driving licence. The race was scheduled to start at Hopkinton, half an hour away from the Pandya home at Needham.

After a little thought, Bonnie agreed and driving swiftly the two somehow reached Hopkinton in time. Giving Sunita ten cents, her mother said, 'Call me if you get tired.' As Sunita started the race, Bonnie drove on to wait at Wellesley, the halfway mark. She didn't expect Sunita to make it there but decided to wait anyway. The runners passed by after sometime and Bonnie kept her eyes peeled for her young daughter. Two hours after the race had started Sunita turned the corner from where Bonnie stood. When she saw her mother, Sunita came to a halt. Taking her shoes—high tops—off, she handed them to Bonnie saying, 'My feet are killing me in these.' And she continued running. Barefoot, she reached the finish line where a proud Bonnie now waited.

It had taken Sunita close to five hours but imagine, no other preparation for the marathon besides her daily dose of swimming. She had run twenty-six miles, completed a full marathon and she was still a teenager! Sunita's parents consider this as one of her biggest achievements to date.

1

The Busy Pandya Family

At half past five, Bonnie Pandya waited, warming up her Ford station wagon. Shortly after, her three children, Jay, Dina and Sunita would troop out of the door and get into the car. Sometimes it'd still be dark but the Pandya kids were always wide awake, even ten-year-old Sunita. She was the youngest of the trio and despite the early hours, she was already chattering happily. Bonnie would then drive her children to the swimming pool at Harvard University where for the next couple of hours they joined the swim team for practice. It was the beginning of what was often a busy, busy day.

The Pandyas, it seemed, never sat still. Mr Pandya—Deepak—was a busy doctor and researcher. Mrs

Pandya—Bonnie—was the busy mom who juggled three jobs, as coordinator at Babson College, teacher of needlework at night at Needham High and as lifeguard at the Babson Recreation Center, while also looking after her home and kids. Every morning she was up at half past four to get ready for the long day ahead. After swim practice, she would drop the children to their schools before heading off to work. At school, Suni and Dina were recognized as 'the girls with the wet hair' as their long, dark hair was often still damp from their morning dip. After school, Bonnie would drive them to Harvard again for a couple of hours of swimming. This routine continued until the three of them graduated from high school. While remembering their childhood, Bonnie says, 'All three were very competitive.'

The Pandya home was in Needham, a Boston suburb, where they lived from 1966 to 1995. The famous universities—Boston University (BU) and Harvard—were close by and Deepak, a neuroanatomist (one who studies the nervous system), himself taught at BU. Sunita was only a year old and Dina and Jay were three and four respectively when the family moved to Boston from Euclid, Ohio. Sunita started her schooling in Needham at the local elementary school. She loved school but she loved the pool more. Ask her about her first time in the water and she doesn't even remember having learnt to swim! It has been a part of her life forever. At first Bonnie would take her to the local YMCA but by the time she was ten Sunita joined Jay and Dina at the Harvard pool where they were coached by the legendary Joe Bernal. Formerly the head coach at Harvard University, Bernal is now an Olympic coach. Sunita, Jay and Dina were a part of his swim club, Bernal's Gators. Until she graduated from high school, Sunita remained in the Bernal's Gators, and for a long time was the youngest Gator on the team.

India, Slovenia and the USA

Deepak Pandya grew up in Jhulasan, a small town near Ahmedabad in Gujarat. He completed his medical studies here. Having lost his parents very early, he chose to follow his older brother, Navin, to the United States. This was in the late 1950s when air travel was still not as common as it is now. For Deepak to reach the United States by sea, he had to travel by train from Jhulasan to Bombay (now Mumbai), from there by ship to London and onward again by another ship, the *Queen Elizabeth*, to New York. The whole journey took twenty-one days! Now compare that with the time it takes now, only a day from Mumbai to New York, or eight and a half minutes to outer space!

Deepak remembers the journey vividly. He says that at the start of his journey, he wasn't very fluent in English. But he met and spoke to so many people on his long voyage across the seas that by the time he arrived in New York, he was speaking English far more confidently than he had starting out!

Deepak's destination was a city called Euclid in the state of Ohio where a job waited for him at the Euclid General Hospital. He thought he would spend two years there and then return to India to practise. Before this period was over, something happened that would change his plans for the future. Ever so often, at the hospital cafeteria, Deepak would run into a young X-ray technician. He never managed to speak to her but found himself glancing her way each time. And one night, at a party, the two of them were introduced for the first time. Her name was Bonnie Zalokar. At the end of the evening, Deepak offered to drop Bonnie home. It was the first time he had a chance to really talk to her. They began dating and were married six months later. It was an intimate church wedding attended by friends, colleagues and relatives of the bride and groom. With this of course, there was no question of Deepak returning to India. The United States became home to the Pandya couple. Deepak continued his residency at the Case Western University, training in neurology.

Bonnie's great-grandparents had emigrated from Slovenia and arrived in America at the turn of the century. Bonnie herself was born and raised in Cleveland, Ohio, where the Zalokar family ran a delicatessen. Food was a big part of their lives and weekends meant getting together as a family, with music and games, over traditional Slovenian food. Bonnie inherited her parents' phenomenal cooking skills. Deepak was vegetarian and after their wedding, Bonnie expanded her culinary repertoire to include vegetarian Gujarati dishes. From the beginning, every meal at the Pandya home included both American and Indian cuisines! Bonnie was also a fantastic baker and later her daughters, too, would often join her. On weekends, Deepak became the chef du jour, whipping up some *pakoras* and *sukhadi*, reminiscent of his childhood in Jhulasan.

Three children were born to Deepak and Bonnie—Jay Thomas, Dina Ann and Sunita Lyn in 1961, 1962 and 1965 respectively. For each child, Neelam, their paternal aunt, chose a name, keeping with the Gujarati tradition.

Bonnie was a practising Catholic and Deepak, a staunch Hindu. Yet there was never a clash of cultures in their home. Both instilled in the children respect for all religions. The whole family went to church on Sundays and Deepak would often carry his Bhagvad Gita with him. They would host visiting swamis from India and with them, conversations tended to be around religion, gods, spirituality and even science. From Deepak too, the kids heard several stories about Ram and Sita, Nala and Damyanti, Savitri, the Mahabharata . . . they were a link to another world, another generation, for Deepak himself had heard them from his mother. There were favourites that the children asked for again and again . . . of the war at Lanka between Ram and Ravan, of Hanuman going in search of the magical Sanjeevani, of Shabari, the tribal woman who waits for Ram in the forest and of course, several tales from the Mahabharata. Christmas and Diwali were important days on the calendar and the Pandyas celebrated both with enthusiasm.

If at home, there was a liberal atmosphere with discussions ranging from philosophy to science, outside things were different. Deepak remembers the 60s and 70s as a difficult period in the States when drug abuse was a growing social problem. He and Bonnie made sure the children were always busy and there was just no time for any distractions. And so, besides several hours of swimming, the kids attended ballet lessons, piano classes, tennis and soccer. And during weekends the whole family would pack up and head to the mountains in their camper!

A love for the outdoors

All the members of the Pandya family enjoyed sports—soccer, tennis, windsurfing, sailing—anything that took them outdoors, really. Camping in the mountains of New Hampshire, even Vermont and Yellowstone, and southwards all the way to Florida—they went everywhere but the Kancamagus Highway was a family favourite. And even here, under the great starry skies, Bonnie would proceed to cook two meals, one American and one Gujarati! In the colder season, the infamous New England winters, the Pandyas would go skiing. And yet there was rarely a day when they missed a swim. Up in the mountains, after a long day on the slopes, the Pandyas would head for the hotel pool!

Without a doubt, Sunita was to the water born. And this is what she loved. By the time she was six years old, she was taking part in various competitions. Her parents remember a swim meet she had attended with friends while her family was away camping. After the meet, she joined them on the campsite. 'How did it go?' they asked. 'Okay,' answered Sunita, without much interest. Later when they looked into her bag, there were five medals from various events.

It did seem like Sunita, more than Dina or Jay was headed for competitive swimming. By the time she was in high school, Sunita's days had come to follow a rigorous routine. Even during holidays, she would go swimming in the morning followed by lifeguarding at Wellesley College. After a quick lunch at home, she would return to her job and then more swim practice with Coach Bernal in the evening. Her day didn't end even then—she was a swim instructor for special-needs kids and only after their session was over did she cycle back home. If Sunita was tired, she didn't show it. Her endurance to finish what she had started would later be of immense help in her chosen work.

Sunita was also always game for adventure, almost as though she wanted to jump in the deep end and figure out how to wade the waters. One year she decided to take part in a swim meet across the Boston Harbor for a marathon swim. The water was freezing cold, filled with jellyfish, and older swimmers were struggling to keep up. Deepak followed Sunita on a boat but even he was amazed by how determined his youngest daughter was. By the time Sunita had finished twelve miles, Deepak decided to pull her out of the water. Only three people went on to complete the marathon and one of them was Jay.

Water held a huge attraction for Sunita—she swam everywhere, at the pool, the lake, at swim-a-thons. Perhaps, thought her friends, she was going to become a swimmer after all!

Go, Rockets!

The mascot of Sunita's school, Needham High, incidentally is a rocket. Talk about interesting coincidences! Since the 1950s, the rocket mascot has occupied a pride of place and the students are often referred to as Needham Rockets; Sunita is perhaps the most famous of them all! More recently, the mascot was given a new image and a new name—Rocky.

2

A Vet in the Making, but Wait, Maybe Not

Almost all of the stories from Sunita's childhood are about her love for swimming. But Sunita herself never thought she would turn into a professional swimmer. It was not an impossible dream but her heart lay elsewhere. In fact, for a long time, Deepak and Bonnie thought that their youngest born would become a vet. Sunita has inherited her mother's love for animals. When she was just five, they got their first family dog for Christmas—a collie named Lassie. In due course, Lassie had a litter and the Pandyas kept one. The tricoloured pup was duly named Bonjo after Bonnie and her mother, Josephine. Over the years the family of collies kept growing with each litter. They became the family that attracted the kids in the neighbourhood and there has barely been a time when the Pandya home didn't ring with happy barks.

At school, Sunita found her interest in the sciences growing. If Ms DiNapoli made 6th grade science fun, Mr Perkins in the 7th grade made it even more exciting! And then there was Ms Piotrowski who encouraged them to grow a garden, and Mr Tomkowitz who took them on a research trip to Cape Cod where they conducted actual experiments in marine biology. All of these people shaped Sunita's thinking and her choices, egging her on to think of a future in the field of science. With a father who was a neuroscientist and teacher-mentors who were clearly shaping her interest in the sciences, and of course, her own love for animals, Sunita began to think that veterinary science was the perfect career choice for her. She graduated from Needham High looking forward to a possible future as an animal doctor.

Sunita sent in her applications and waited to hear about her college admission. One of her options was the acclaimed Columbia University but New York, she reminisces, seemed rather intimidating. Sunita was a New England girl, most comfortable in the university suburbs. Dina was already at Smith College, in Massachusetts, and Jay had opted for the US Naval Academy (USNA).

Even as Sunita was figuring out her plans for college, Jay's graduation came around. The whole family drove to Maryland where Jay proudly showed them around the campus. He also urged Sunita to apply to the USNA. Jay thought it would be a great place for her athletic pursuits; he had himself gone on to captain the academy swim team. Sunita was definitely tempted. She weighed the pros and cons—it would mean she would have to give up her cherished dream of becoming a vet. But she could still pursue the sciences. She would also have to cut her long hair short since those were the rules for naval training. But she would also be one of the few women who, at that time, applied to the Academy. Incidentally, in the year Jay joined the USNA, the first batch of women graduated from there. So it was still very new for women to be in the armed forces. If she could get in, Sunita thought, it would be pretty exciting. Her usual good cheer didn't allow her to wallow in the loss of one dream. Instead she looked forward to the new road ahead.

All applications to the USNA had to be endorsed by a congressman or senator and at that time, the Massachusetts senator was Edward Kennedy. Sunita's application was impressive—she seemed like such an enthusiastic young girl, active in athletics, great at academics, a lifeguard, a 'candy striper' (hospital volunteer). On all accounts she seemed to fit the bill. Her application went through easily. Sunita was accepted into the USNA and she entered the Academy in the summer of 1983, with short-cropped hair, one of a hundred or so women in a class of thousand!

Plebes, youngsters, second class and firsties—four years in the USNA

The plebe summer is the first six weeks of first-year life at the Academy. It is a gruelling period that all candidates have to go through before they actually begin the academic year. It is also a transition period between civilian and military life. About a thousand plebes enter the Academy each year. They are divided into fifteen companies, made up of two platoons each, which in turn have four squads of ten plebes each. During the plebe summer, each squad works together as a team. At the end of this period, the plebes are sworn into the Navy as midshipmen.

Sunita with her swimming prowess made an impact during the plebe summer, winning recognition as an athlete as well as an award for endurance. She was already enjoying the challenge of being here—it was regimental, far more than say, Smith College where Dina was studying. But Sunita found that the system suited her rather well. The years of waking up at the crack of dawn for swim practice were now proving useful. Sunita's days began as early as before. The Academy was preparing its students for a life in the military and demanded nothing short of absolute commitment from them. Sunita reminisces, 'So there I was at the Naval Academy with a lot shorter hair and learning how to march, it was a little bit of a surprise for me but I blended in pretty quickly, and I really had fun and I learned about leadership and followership going through the ranks there, and teamwork. I was on the swim team there, I was on the cross-country team, on the bike club, so a lot of sports, like my brother suggested. I went to jump school and stuff like that, just a lot of good outdoorsy stuff . . .'

Perhaps, Sunita's challenge lay in juggling them all—athletics, academics and a demanding social life! Managing time proved to be the biggest challenge but as teenagers generally do, she coped remarkably well. In the second year at the Academy, students could choose their majors. Sunita opted for Naval Architecture but before the year was over, she realized that it was proving more than she could handle given everything else she was doing. She withdrew from Naval Architecture, transferring to a General Sciences major. In 1987, Sunita graduated from the Navy, with the rank of ensign.

Sunita says she was not a class topper, but her achievements are nevertheless significant—like Jay and Dina, she too captained the college swim team and was on the cross-country and biking teams. Now as ensign, she had the choice of entering surface line, navy air, marine or submarine for service. It was the 'specials' that caught her fancy. Navy Diving and Navy Air were the specialized programmes and Sunita, with her keen interest in swimming, didn't think twice—she applied for Navy Diving. The application didn't go through. To her dismay, there was only one opening and it was not offered to her. She decided to go for Navy Air. It was the second time in her life that Sunita found herself missing out on her first choice. She had to settle for an alternative option and learn to love it. But what a stroke of chance, a play of destiny it turned out to be, for it put her firmly on the path to becoming an astronaut.

As it turned out, while waiting for her air training to begin, a spot opened up for diving and Sunita took it. She spent the next six months working hard to earn a Basic Diving Officer Certificate. With this done, she reported to the Naval Aviation Training Command to begin her training to fly. Once more, she found that while her first choice was combat aircraft, she had to choose the helicopter. Looking back, Sunita recounts, 'It was the time of *Top Gun*, so I wanted to be a jet pilot. That didn't pan out either. I became a helicopter pilot. But I found that I really loved flying helicopters. I loved working on helicopters. I loved the crew concept and the teamwork with the crewmen in the back.'

Sunita soon realized that she loved flying. It almost came to rival her passion for swimming. On completing her aviator training, she was assigned to the Helicopter Combat Support Squadron 8 at Virginia. While here, her deployments took her to the Mediterranean, the

Red Sea and the Persian Gulf. During this time, she carried supplies and cargo during the Gulf War of 1990 as part of Operation Desert Shield in Saudi Arabia and Operation Provide Comfort in Iraq, and later to Miami, Florida, for Hurricane Andrew Relief Operations. Sunita Pandya was now a full-fledged Naval Pilot.

With all the flying hours she was logging, Sunita's next destination was the Naval Test Pilot School at Maryland. It was a matter of great pride to be granted admission there for the selection process was highly competitive. In January 1993, Sunita began her year-long course towards becoming a test pilot. She was now flying all kinds of aircraft: the H-46, the V-22 Osprey, T-2 Buckeye, the SH-60 Seahawk, the UH-1 Iroquois, the AH-1 SuperCobra, the SH-2 Seasprite, the SH-3 Sea King, the CH-53 E Sea Stallion, the H-57 Sea Ranger. For someone who loved helicopters, testing those that were yet to be launched was nothing short of exhilarating! In 1995, she returned to the flight school as an instructor in the Rotary Wing department. By this time she had logged almost 3000 flight hours in over thirty different aircraft—the once prolific swimmer was well and truly airborne!

The Herndon Climb

At the USNA there is a tall obelisk, a monument to Captain William Lewis Herndon who was the commander of the steamer, the SS *Central America*. In September 1857, on a journey from Cuba towards the East Coast of America this vessel was caught in a hurricane. Captain Herndon arranged for the women and children on board to be rescued in lifeboats. But there was simply no way of saving all the passengers and crew. Herndon remained on board the ship and drowned along with over 400 others. It was, one of the largest losses in the history of sea travel. In Herndon's memory, the USNA Class of 1860 erected a granite obelisk on the grounds of the naval academy. Beginning 1959 a tradition was established where the plebe year ends with an attempt by the plebes to scale the obelisk. The one who reaches the top will take down the plebe Dixie cup cap and replace it with a peaked midshipman cap. This is a 'plebes-no-more' ceremony, bringing an end to the first year. The monument is slathered with lard to make it very slippery and tricky to climb. The plebes make a team and attempt to send a representative all the way up. In Sunita's time, she was the only woman who attempted to climb the obelisk. Sunita slithered halfway up the obelisk before she was pulled down by the senior students.

3

'I Can Fly a Copter, Maybe I Can Go to Space'

Happenstance—that's how Sunita describes the events in her life—the curvy paths that she has had to take that have often sprung surprises. Again and again in her life, Sunita found that her number one choices were eluding her but her alternative choices were turning out to be more interesting and taking her along rather unusual but exciting paths. The adventure, it seemed, had only just begun!

While preparing to be a test pilot, Sunita visited the Johnson Space Center in Houston, Texas. This was mandatory for all test pilot students. Sunita flew down for a session with John Young who had had a long and illustrious career as an astronaut. He had been on six space flights, was the ninth person to land on the Moon and had actually travelled to it twice (once even driving a lunar vehicle on its surface!). So, sitting in the class, listening to Young talk about his experiences was a wonderful opportunity. Sunita, listening with rapt attention, heard one thing ring aloud: this renowned astronaut had to learn to fly helicopters to prepare for his Moon landing. It set Sunita thinking, 'I can fly a helicopter. Maybe I too can go to space!' And the more Sunita considered it, the more plausible it seemed. Sunita says she didn't really know much about the space programme and what it involved but to her it seemed a bit like being a test pilot. You have a test plan, a programme, do the tests, come back and see how the results can make it better. Astronauts, she figured, went to space, did some experiments, fed the results to people who used it to improve things or learn more. It was a perfect fit for someone with her qualifications and interest.

Incidentally the USNA is credited with sending the highest number of students to the astronaut programme, so much so that they now have an

Astronaut Convocation Day when alumni are invited to speak to present pupils. Furthermore, top-ranking students from the Naval Test Pilot School that Sunita had attended often opted for the astronaut programme. So, perhaps, Sunita's choices were not so far-fetched after all.

She sent her application to NASA but it was, as she had feared, rejected. NASA receives thousands of entries and to be considered, one has to qualify at several levels. Applicants rarely find themselves accepted on the first attempt. So although it was disappointing, she wasn't going to give up just yet. The astronaut bug had bitten Sunita. She knew that she needed to equip herself with a Master's Degree and in 1993, after finishing at the Test Pilot School, she entered the Florida Institute of Technology for a two-year programme in Engineering Management. Graduating in 1995, Sunita could now think of reapplying to NASA. She also returned to the Test Pilot School as instructor, logging in more flight hours and working to build a rock-solid resume. When she finally resent her application to NASA in 1997, it was indeed looking good:

- Physical Fitness ✔
- Academic Qualifications ✔
- At least 1000 hours of flying ✔
- Team Player ✔
- Not Claustrophobic ✔
- Ready for Adventure ✔

Sunita was among the lucky few to find her application going through on the second attempt itself. It was indeed a cause for celebration! In the summer of 1998, while she was assigned to the ship USS *Saipan*, which was at Norfolk, Virginia, at that time, Sunita received 'the call' from the Astronaut Office in Houston. She was asked to come down for an interview. Sunita's life was about to change once more. She was selected to be an astronaut-in-training. She moved to Houston, eager to embark on a new dream.

Sunita was now an engineer, a diver, a helicopter pilot, a test pilot and astronaut-in-training! Looking at her own life, Sunita offers some advice, 'Don't be afraid to fail, because you find out a little more about yourself when you don't get your first choice and then you end up finding something that you will do well because you like it. When you like something, you will do it well and then you're going to get the rewards at the end.'

Meanwhile, life continued . . .

One of Sunita's batchmates from the Academy was a young man named Michael Williams. After graduating, they went their own ways and lost touch. It was a friend's wedding at Pensacola, Florida, a couple of years later that Sunita and Michael met once again. They spent the day catching up on their lives and enjoyed each other's company so much they knew that they just had to meet again. And again. Sunita describes Michael as a straight-laced and dependable guy. They dated for two years. Towards the end of their flight school, Sunita and Michael decided to get married. Their wedding took place in a beautiful old church in Woods Hole, Massachusetts. Sunita wore a long white gown and Michael looked every inch a naval officer in his stripes. Dina was the maid of honour and Sunita's friends from the Academy, Heidi Moser, Debbie Klatt and Vicky Webster were her bridesmaids. A proud Deepak walked his daughter down the aisle. Friends and relatives from across the United States and from Europe and India attended the ceremony.

Soon after the wedding, Sunita and Michael moved to Virginia where they awaited their deployment. Michael too was assigned to the Helicopter Combat Support Squadron but the rules did not permit a married couple to be on the same ship. For the newly-weds, finding time together was a challenge. Sunita says, 'When we were not deployed, life was almost normal. We worked eight-hour days at the office but by this time we had two dogs and one of us would make it a point to be home at night for them. Life was as normal as it could be.'

A few years later Michael left the Navy to become a Federal Marshal while Sunita who had once imagined she would be a Squadron Commanding Officer in faraway Italy looked even further—spacewards.

India's First Man in Space

India sent its first astronaut to space in the early 80s. The lucky man was Wing Commander Rakesh Sharma, a test pilot with the Indian Air Force. Rakesh was born in Patiala, in Punjab, on 3 January 1949. In 1960, he enrolled at the National Defence Academy as an IAF cadet and in 1970 joined the Air Force as a pilot officer. When the Soviet Interkosmos programme and the Indian Space Research Organization came together, Rakesh Sharma, then a Squadron Leader, was selected as India's representative. For over a year, Rakesh trained in the Soviet Union. On 3 April 1984, along with two Russian cosmonauts, he launched into space on the Soyuz T11. He spent almost eight days on the Salyut 7 Space Station that orbited Earth from 1982 to 1991. While in space, Rakesh conducted many experiments for the Indian space research programme. The then Prime Minister, Indira Gandhi, got to speak to him while he was there. She is said to have asked him how India looked from space, and he replied famously, 'Sare jahaan se acha, hindustan hamara.'

Rakesh Sharma was honoured with Hero of the Soviet Union, and the Ashoka Chakra.

A Brief History of Space Travel

To really understand what Sunita was getting into, we'll digress a bit to understand what space travel is all about. The urge to explore and seek new frontiers has always driven man from earliest times. And when he had explored the length and breadth of Earth, and of the seas, the skies beckoned. It was in the years after the Second World War that space travel gathered momentum. This was the time of the Cold War between the two superpowers that reigned—the United States and the Union of Soviet Socialist Republics (USSR). Even the space programme became a point of contention leading to The Space Race! Everything was done in secret by both these countries. The Soviet Union made great inroads in space exploration, when they launched *Sputnik 1* on 1 October 1957, marking the dawn of the space age. They kept it up with more satellites to orbit the Moon. All of these, of course, had no human beings on them. These were still baby steps towards space travel.

★ Laika and other animals in space

Before scientists could imagine sending man up into space, they decided to send animals up to test the effects of microgravity. There are conflicting opinions about whether this is ethical or not and like so many science experiments that use animals for research this too is part of the debate. In November 1957, the USSR sent up a dog named Laika on *Sputnik 2*. But she was not the first non-human in space. Fruit flies had been launched on a captured Nazi rocket in the late 1940s; they went up about a 100 km before they were rescued with a parachute. And then it was the turn of the monkeys. Four monkeys, all named Albert, were sent up at different times. Each of them died when their rockets failed. It was then the turn of mice in the early 1950s. They too didn't survive.

But Laika was special. She had been picked up from the streets of Russia and deemed suitable since as a stray she was hardy and hence thought to be able to face challenges. Along with two other dogs,

Albina and Mushka, Laika underwent space training—living in a confined space, being placed in simulators to familiarize them with the noise of the spacecraft, and eating food that was offered in a gelatinous form. Of these three dogs, Laika was eventually chosen to fly. She was going to be launched on the *Sputnik 2*, which had an oxygen generator along with equipment that could prevent oxygen overload and allow for carbon dioxide absorption. A fan to prevent the cabin from overheating and food to last at least seven days was also provided. Laika was fitted with a bag to collect waste and also had sensors attached to her to measure her breathing, pulse and blood pressure. Laika became the first living being to orbit Earth. *Sputnik 2* remained in orbit for five months but Laika didn't make it back alive. Reports vary about her actual time of death but in the recent years, it has been confirmed that she died from cabin overheating within hours of being in space. A monument to Laika stands in Russia, in honour of world's first astronaut.

There was an uproar in parts of the world about animal abuse but sadly, the ongoing Cold War and the political one-upmanship that the USSR and the US were vying for overshadowed the protests of animal lovers. But the USSR was not alone in using animals in space programmes. The USA used chimpanzees. The Holloman Airforce Base had forty chimpanzees, all potential candidates for the space programme. This eventually reduced to six 'astro-chimps', and each was recognized by a number, and not given a name. It was Number 65 (aka Chop Chop Chang by his handlers) who flew on the Mercury-Redstone 2 or MR-2 Mission in 1961. Number 65 was trained to pull levers—a right hand lever when a white light came on and a left hand lever for a blue light. By doing so in space, he proved that tasks could be accomplished in a microgravity environment. The chimp spent sixteen minutes and thirty-nine seconds in space before the capsule landed in the Atlantic and was rescued. Besides a bruised nose, Number 65 was safe and his successful return earned him a name—Ham—so called after the Holloman Aerospace Medical Center. Ham was now a hero! *LIFE* magazine reported, 'When Ham's capsule was opened at sea after the flight, first a hand was thrust out to shake the anxious vet's, then Ham stepped out, burping proudly.'

In the USSR, it was *Sputnik 5* that managed to successfully bring back the animals alive—dogs Belka and Strelka along with a gray rabbit, two rats, forty-two mice and several fruit flies. Veterok and

Ugalyok hold the record for the longest space flight by dogs: twenty-two days in orbit before landing safely on 16 March 1966.

Animals continue to make space trips and are now called biological payloads.

⋆ Manned satellites or satellites with men aboard

Although animals were being launched regularly, most were still 'suborbital' space flights, which means that although they are launched with enough force to get them to 100 km above sea level, the speed is not sufficient for the vehicle to go around Earth. More acceleration is required to propel a rocket for orbit. The suborbital vehicles fall back to Earth after reaching their highest point. The USSR was making great progress in orbital space flights and was the first country to send man into space. Twenty hand-picked pilots were being trained for space flights by the USSR. They were tested on several levels before the twenty-seven-year-old, 5'2' tall Yuri Gagarin was selected. Being short is of significance since the *Vostok* that he would fly in had little space and only a small person could fit in it reasonably comfortably. On 12 April 1961, Yuri Gagarin climbed aboard the *Vostok 1* and went around Earth. He spent 108 minutes in space. History was made! Man had taken a significant step in his exploration of a new frontier.

In the US, the success of Ham's flight propelled a human suborbital flight. A new agency, the National Aeronautics and Space Administration (NASA), had been established in 1958. It took the lead on the American space programme and military test pilots were invited to train here for space flights to be conducted with humans abroad. Within months of Ham's return, Alan Shepard became the first American in space. On 5 May 1961, Shepard was launched by another Redstone rocket and he reached a distance of 187 km before returning to Earth. It was a fifteen-minute suborbital space flight and the highlight of the trip was that Shepard could manually manoeuvre the craft at a certain altitude.

Both US and USSR now began to work on manned space flights. In 1962, John Glenn became the first American to orbit Earth. In 1963, Valentina Tereshkova was the first woman to go to space. In 1965, Aleksei Leonov performed a spacewalk. In 1969, the Americans sent the *Apollo 11* to the Moon with Neil Armstrong and Edwin Aldrin. In the decades that followed, the US and USSR were actively competing in the progress and success of their space programmes. But perhaps credit must be given to the Soviets for the many firsts they achieved—the first space shuttle, the first spacewalk, and soon the first space station.

⋆ Space stations

Man was now flying with increased regularity to space. But to take the programme to the next step was a challenge. How could astronauts spend time in space? There are no homestays here, no motels, no cousins or aunts to stay with, no lodges or five-stars. You can't pitch a tent and rough it out either. So where could they stay?

The plan was to construct and launch a space station that becomes a home/hotel for visiting space travellers. The USSR built the *Salyut 1* and launched it in April 1971. The *Salyut 1* was sixty-five feet long and thirteen feet wide at its widest point. It was cylindrical and had three compartments for astronauts and one for the engine and controls. At either end was a double set of solar panels, extending out like wings. Two days after the *Salyut 1* was launched, the rocket *Soyuz 10* was sent up with three cosmonauts. They were to spend thirty days on *Salyut 1*. The Soyuz was to dock at the space station, which means that the two vehicles would connect with each other when a hatch door would open to allow the cosmonauts to move from the rocket to the space station. *Soyuz 10* was unable to dock at the station and so had to return to Earth much earlier than planned. On 6 June of the same year, *Soyuz 11* went up carrying three other cosmonauts. They successfully docked at the station and spent twenty-two days in orbit, going around Earth 383 times! On 29 June, the cosmonauts shifted back to the Soyuz and began their return. Unfortunately at that time, cosmonauts did not wear their spacesuits in flight and what happened was that the pressure inside the cabin dropped on re-entry. So although the vehicle landed safely, the three cosmonauts were dead, due to asphyxiation or lack of sufficient oxygen.

It was a big blow to the space programme and called for new designs, especially to ensure that on re-entry, safety could be ensured. The *Salyut 1* remained in orbit until October that year and on the 11th of the month, the station was brought lower into the atmosphere and then it plunged into the Pacific Ocean. Until 1986, several versions of the *Salyut* were launched into space and with each one, there was more improvement and newer features. All of them were short-term space stations. NASA sent up the Skylab that orbited Earth between 1973 and 1979 and supported manned missions.

The next stage of space stations was the Mir. Unlike the Salyuts, it was made of modules which means that rather than being one large unit, it had several components that were assembled over ten years. In 1986 the core module was launched and over the next decade, six other modules were launched and attached to the core. When completed, it weighed 1,29,700 kg and was 62.3 feet long, 101.7 feet wide and 90.2 feet high. Between 1986 and 2001, it orbited between 296 and 421 kms above Earth—considered the low Earth orbit. Of the fifteen years that it remained in space, it was occupied by visiting cosmonauts for over twelve years.

This was the start of long-duration space trips and also allowed for experiments aboard the space station.

By the early 1990s the Cold War had thawed between the two countries. The USSR dissolved in 1991 into several democratic republics. Mir was now owned by Russia. In the decade that followed, the Mir became the space station accessed by over a hundred cosmonauts and astronauts from twelve countries, including the USSR/Russia, and USA. Between January 1994 and March 1995 Cosmonaut Valeri Polyakov spent 437 days and eighteen hours aboard Mir, creating a record for the longest human space flight (a record that has since been broken twice).

On 23 March 2001, setting the record for the longest single human space flight, the Mir returned to Earth, crashing into the South Pacific Ocean.

⋆ Baikonur

For a long time, Baikonur, the site of the Soviet space programme, remained a secret city. It used to be called Leninsk until 1995, and it had been chosen for several reasons—it is surrounded by plains (perfect for uninterrupted radio signals), is away from people, and is close to the equator (which makes for a high rotational axis, our planet being spherical). A cosmodrome was constructed that would facilitate all space launches, and to support this structure, a city was built around it. Those who worked on the space programmes moved here with their families. Homes, schools, a hospital, markets, a railway station and also an airport . . . everything came up. Baikonur or rather Leninsk became the space town.

With the dissolution of the Soviet in 1991, Baikonur went to Kazakhstan but Russia opted to lease the cosmodrome from Kazakhstan in order to continue its space programme. Today, Baikonur continues to play an important part in the space programme, and is the launch site for all manned vehicles to the International Space Station. For space fans, Baikonur is absolute heaven. You can stay at the Cosmos Hotel and spend your time looking at launch pads, visiting the space museum and if you have scheduled to see a rocket launch, that too is possible!

Cosmonaut or Astronaut?

When NASA was formed, its programme director wanted to give a name to the space flight pilots. An appropriate word had to be coined. One suggestion was Mercury, after the Roman messenger god. But the name Mercury had already been used for the earlier space programme. Allen Gamble, who worked at NASA between 1958 and 1964, says, 'With our best name so far already taken, out came the dictionaries and thesauruses. Someone found that the term aeronaut, referring to those who ride in balloons and other lighter-than-air vehicles, was derived from "sailor in the air". From this we arrived at astronaut, meaning "sailor among the stars."'

The Soviets were not far behind in this space race. They came up with the name 'cosmonaut' or 'sailor of the universe'.

Incidentally, the Chinese astronauts are called taikonauts and the Indian astronauts will be called vyomanauts from the Sanskrit 'vyom' meaning space.

Houston Calling Sunita!

Sunita's father, Deepak, remembers the Moon landing in 1969. He was watching Neil Armstrong set foot on the lunar surface on TV. Four-year-old Sunita sat on his lap and jumped up and down with glee! Fast forward to 1998, when a thirty-three-year-old Sunita walked into NASA's Johnson Space Center as an astronaut-in-training. She had travelled far from Needham through Maryland and Florida to Houston and now was set to reach beyond Earth!

All astronauts-in-training have to spend two and a half years in, as you may have guessed, training before they can be called Astronauts. In the first month of training itself, all of them must clear a swimming test, swimming in a twenty-five metre pool—three lengths first and then three more lengths wearing a flight suit and swimming shoes! Even for an ace swimmer like Sunita, this was quite a challenge. No two days of training were the same—sometimes it was a classroom session and other times, they were placed in simulators, which means that they existed within a version of the actual space station. They became familiar with how it looked and even with the microgravity environment. They performed repairs, maintenance and gained skill in all their tasks. Everything they would do in space was practised extensively here.

By the time Sunita started her training several developments had taken place. The United States lacked the budget to complete the design and development of its proposed space station, Freedom. Its construction was definitely not cheap and politicians questioned the spending of so many billions on it. In 1993, when Bill Clinton was President, USA had decided to abandon working on its own space station and instead joined hands with other countries towards building a common space station. The Russians had been building Mir 2, the Europeans were setting up Columbus (named after Christopher Columbus!), and the Japanese were constructing the Kibo. The US and Russia along with the other countries now came together in one of the twentieth century's most significant act of international unity—the construction of the International Space Station (ISS). The Cold War was over.

When Sunita joined NASA, five years had passed since the plan for ISS had been formulated. Russia and the US had been busy at work in the construction of the required modules or the parts that would form the ISS. Like the earlier Mir, the ISS was going to be a modular space station and the construction was expected to take several years. Delays were inevitable—it was a huge project after all. Finally it seemed that the first of the modules that would become the start of the ISS was ready for launch—the rocket Proton would carry the Russian module, Zarya on 20 November 1998, from Baikonur. Once Zarya was placed in orbit NASA prepared for the launch of its module, Unity. The module was carried by the SS *Endeavour*—one of the five space shuttles that NASA owned. *Endeavour* also carried two astronauts—James Newman and Jerry Ross. They set out on an EVA or Extravehicular Activity or in simple terms, a spacewalk, during which they connected Unity with Zarya. It was the first ever EVA from the ISS.

Sunita watched history taking place from her privileged place as a NASA astronaut. Her training now included sessions with those who had earlier gone on the mission. She couldn't wait for her turn to come. As a test pilot, Sunita was preparing to go as Flight Engineer on her mission. She was training in robotics, spacewalks and the Russian language while also familiarizing herself with the Russian module.

A mission-specific training also allowed the astronauts to get to know and work with each other. Perhaps the hardest part of a long duration mission is for an astronaut to live and work with a few crewmates in a closed and isolated place. Imagine, if you get angry, you cannot just storm out and bang the door shut. You cannot call a friend and crib for an hour (phone calls are possible but also expensive)! You cannot go shopping or to the movies or order pizza and binge eat. You have to learn to live and work on a small team and there really is no room for claustrophobia. And so, among the things that astronauts do during training is the NASA Extreme Environment Mission Operations or NEEMO. Here, the astronauts are sent underwater to the Aquarius, an undersea research station, one-of-its-kind in the world.

Sunita spent nine days underwater on the Aquarius as part of her training. This is considered to simulate the environment in space—hostile, alien and tough. Anyone with even the slightest degree of claustrophobia would probably baulk at this but it offers a realistic view of what to expect while in space. Preparing for a microgravity situation is another thing the astronauts are exposed to everyday. As a pilot, Sunita continued to log flying hours and, of course, swimming remained an essential part of her daily routine. These were busy, exciting days and Sunita knew that in only a few years, she could be on the space shuttle, living her dream.

Meanwhile, the missions to the ISS continued with the Russian Zvezda that was launched in 2000. From this point, the ISS was inhabitable and at least two astronauts could man it. Missions were launched at regular intervals that carried several modules to construct the ISS. The space mission was progressing well.

Star City, Russia

What was once called 'Closed Military Townlet 1' during the Cold War days is today the cheerful sounding Star City. Located in Moscow, it's where the Yuri Gagarin

Cosmonaut Training Center is situated. The Cosmonaut Training Center is over half a century old and Star City itself is home to several cosmonauts and their families. Although most people training here have been from the Soviet Union and now Russia, it has increasingly become a place for astronauts from all over the world. NASA crew first came here in 1973 but it was only in 1994 that they made their presence here more permanent when two astronauts arrived here to train for a Mir mission. Today, NASA astronauts spend several months in Star City. All of them learn Russian. Sunita herself is a regular at Star City and speaks Russian fairly fluently. When she adopted a Jack Rusell terrier, she named him Gorby after the last of the Soviet Presidents, Mikhail Gorbachev.

Preparing for flight

Sunita's astronaut training progressed steadily. She expected her first space flight to take place in a matter of four to five years and was looking forward to it. In the winter of 2002, Charlie Precourt, the Chief of the Astronaut Office, informed Sunita that she had been selected for a mission. Meanwhile, an Indian-born aerospace engineer named Kalpana Chawla was training as a Mission

Specialist to launch in the SS *Columbia*, on 16 January 2003. There was to be a seven-member crew of Michael Anderson, David Brown, Rick Husband, Laurel Clark, William McCool and Ilan Ramon besides Kalpana. They were scheduled to spend sixteen days on the ISS. After a successful mission, the SS *Columbia* began its re-entry as scheduled. However, on entering Earth's atmosphere, the shuttle caught fire and disintegrated, killing all seven abroad. It turns out that when the space shuttle launched, some of the foam insulation that protected it from heat fell off on to the left wing. The thermal protection system was damaged and when the shuttle re-entered Earth's atmosphere, hot gases entered the wing leading to the fatal accident. It was one of the biggest blows to the space programme. Sunita was in Hawaii when she heard of the tragedy. It devastated her. 'I lost seven friends that day,' she recalls in grief.

Following the accident, NASA's remaining space shuttles were grounded. Space operations were delayed. The construction of the ISS was put on hold from the American side. It also meant that Sunita would not go to space as scheduled. The 1998-ers, Group 17 of the astronauts-in-training of whom Sunita was a part, called themselves the Penguins—the flightless birds. And of them, Sunita wrote in her blog: 'Patience is a virtue, I think, all of us have.'

It was only in 2005 that operations resumed with the shuttle SS *Discovery*. Sunita was now scheduled for a space mission in 2006, eight years after she had entered NASA. The launch was to be on 9 December 2006. Deepak, Bonnie, Michael and Dina arrived at Cape Canaveral in Florida. Other relatives also joined, some from Ohio and others from as far as India. The Pandyas and Zalokars were in full attendance. For one week before take off, the astronauts are in quarantine i.e. their contact with people is restricted. This is done to prevent them from catching any viruses. Falling sick on the ISS can be uncomfortable, inconvenient and just a big problem! Deepak remembers, 'We saw her just before lift off but by this time they were already in quarantine and we had to keep a distance. She talked to us, said namaste to everyone. A Hindu priest had been invited and he said a mantra for her safe trip. The launch was postponed by a day because of clouds. When we saw her next, she was on the space shuttle, right on top. We sat watching. The countdown started. There was a huge glow and then the shuttle blasted with a big, thundering noise. All of us were praying. Later we saw a video of Sunita during the launch and she looked so happy.'

An Inspiration Named Kalpana

Kalpana Chawla's story is both inspiring and heartbreaking. Growing up in Karnal in Haryana, Kalpana did her schooling there at the Tagore Public School, graduating in 1976. She followed that with a Bachelor's in aerospace engineering from the Punjab Engineering College in Chandigarh (1982). From here on, her career was shaped in the US where she moved to do her post-graduation in aerospace engineering from the University of Texas at Arlington (1984). One more Master's degree followed and then she went on to earn a PhD in aerospace engineering from the University of Colorado at Boulder (1988).

The desire to work with airplanes came early, from watching the crafts in Karnal. It was one of the few towns in the country that actually have a flying club where Pushpak airplanes and gliders are regularly flown. Kalpana and her brother would sometimes ask their father to get them a ride in one of the planes and he would oblige by taking them to the club. Kalpana loved flying so much that she trained and became a certified flight instructor and held a commercial pilot's licence for single and multi engine land and seaplanes and gliders.

On completing her PhD, Kalpana joined NASA where she worked at the Ames Research Center in California. Five years later, she joined Overset Methods Inc as Vice President and Research Scientist. When NASA selected her as an astronaut candidate in December 1994, she reported to the Johnson Space Center. Her first flight was *on* SS *Columbus* between 19 November and 5 December 1997. She was a Mission Specialist and her job was to operate the shuttle's robot arm. In 2003, she returned to space on SS *Columbia* once more. The shuttle took off on 16 January 2003 and was scheduled to return on 1 February of the same year. On re-entry, it disintegrated killing all crew. 'None of our astronauts travelled a longer path to space than Kalpana Chawla,' then US President George W. Bush said. 'She left India as a student but she would see the nation of her birth, all of it, from hundreds of miles above.'

Kalpana and Sunita were colleagues and friends. By the time Sunita arrived in Houston in 1997, Kalpana had already travelled to space once.

Sunita with her parents, Dina and Gorby

Dina comes visiting to the USNA in 1983, at the end of the plebe summer

Sunita with her mother, Bonnie Pandya, taken on a visit to Slovenia

Sunita with her father, Dr Deepak Pandya, in New Hampshire

Sunita loves baseball! Here she's with her friend Terry Ravanis and Red Sox star Jerry Remmy at a Boston Red Sox Game.

Bonnie, Dina and Sunita at Jay's graduation from the USNA

Sunita with the USNA cross-country team

Running—her life-long passion

Dina (17) and Sunita (14) as Bernal's Gators!

A family of dog lovers—Sunita and Bonnie with Gorby and Coal at Falmouth

Dressed in ethnic finery on an Indian holiday

Elephant rides and a visit to the Taj Mahal
were definitely on the Indian itinerary

Deepak and Bonnie's 40th wedding anniversary at
Falmouth Beach in 2001. Sunita, Michael, Jay,
Anna (Jay's wife), Dina, Bonnie and Deepak with Coal

Sunita with Gorby and Elsie, Dina's dog

Just married, Mr and Mrs Williams!

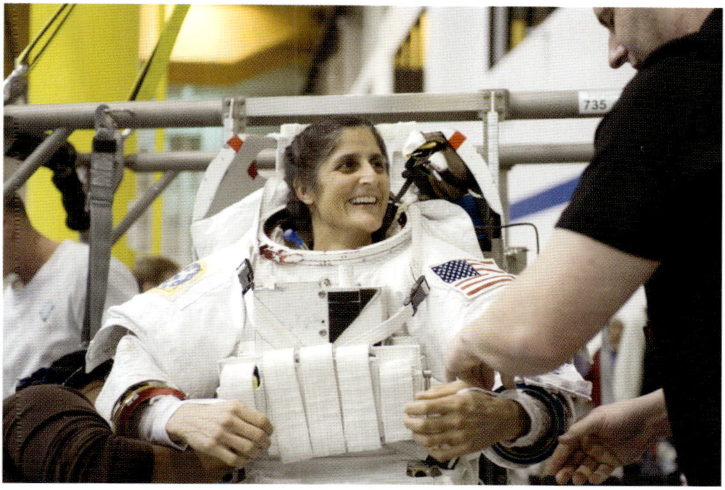

At Johnson Space Center

Practising the spacewalk in the waters
of the Neutral Buoyancy Lab at the JSC

Dressed and ready for a spacewalk!

Sunita gives a thumbs up to the media at
Gagarin Cosmonaut Training Center in Star City, Russia

The *Soyuz TMA-05M* launches from Baikonur carrying Sunita, Yuri and Aki on 15 July 2012

Sunita exercising on the Cycle Ergometer with
Vibration Isolation System aka CEVIS

Sunita training on the Combined Operational Load Bearing
External Resistance Treadmill aka COLBERT on the ISS

Just another day at the office

Floating in the ISS

Sunita and Aki work the controls at the robotics workstation in the Cuppola

Sunita on her second EVA during the
construction of the ISS. That's Earth behind her!

This is how the landing chute looks as it approaches Earth

Inside the spacecraft

Sunita being felicitated by the Gujarati
Association after her first space mission

Which Way to the International Space Station?

During her space sojourn Sunita maintained a detailed blog. It reads like a fascinating diary. Of the launch, she wrote, 'Getting into space is quite a jolt! Needless to say, besides your brain, the rest of the body takes some time to adjust. The first six hours of being in-orbit were a little difficult. I think things just didn't know where to go . . . The auxiliary power units start up, the vehicle begins vibrating and we are thinking, we are really going to go this time! Six seconds before launch, the main engines start and we are rumbling and shaking pretty significantly. Now it seemed like we were really, really going to go. Then the blast of the solid rocket boosters launched us right off the pad. I don't think my stomach knew what was going on at all!

'We started to accelerate like nobody's business . . . our stomachs and the rest of us are really getting squished now . . . we were still accelerating through the thinning of the atmosphere. Then everything got quiet. My pen started to float and my arms started to float . . .

'We were hooting and hollering the entire time . . . Joanie, Christer and I were all three shaking hands and shouting for the entire ride, sort of like screaming on a roller coaster. When we were there, we couldn't stop laughing!'

The shuttle takes all of eight minutes to be launched into space. Once outside Earth's orbit, it begins to circle our planet before docking. It has to dock at the ISS, which is cruising around Earth at the rate of 17,500 miles an hour. That's seven-something kms a second! So the ISS is certainly not stationary. And then of course, it's a big sky and the space shuttle has to locate the ISS before it can dock there for its crew to land. So who gives the shuttle directions to the ISS? The Launch Control team monitor the launch of the shuttle; the launch times and lift off are planned so that when the shuttle reaches space, it's ahead of the ISS orbiting over that point, which happens twice a day for ten minutes. The launch has to happen within a given time frame. Once it does, the space shuttle will begin to orbit around Earth. The average time to dock at the ISS used to be two days. Since March 2013, docking times have reduced to six hours, making same-day launch and docking a much-welcomed reality.

The space shuttles can carry up to seven astronauts and along with Sunita were Mark Polansky (Commander), Mission Specialists Joan Higginbotham, Nicholas Patrick, Christer Fuglesang, Robert Curbeam and Pilot William Oefelein. All of them, except Sunita, were on a twelve-day mission to work on the construction of the ISS. They were scheduled to return before Christmas. Sunita, on the other hand, was part of the longer-duration Expedition 14. Its Commander was Michael Lopez Alegria or LA as he was called and her other crewmate was Mikhail Tyurin or Misha. LA and Misha had arrived on 20 September 2006 on a Soyuz from Baikonur and were already there when Sunita arrived on the SS *Discovery*.

Houston, can you hear me?

Once the shuttle had docked and the crew could connect with the station and prepare to enter the ISS, Sunita found that she would need floating practice! She kept banging into corners and things but so did all the others. The crew began preparing for their stay in space, setting a net for the spacesuits, getting out of it and helping the others out of it, rolling out of sleeping bags . . . regular unpacking! Mark Polansky called for Sunita to arrive at the deck for her astronaut wings, another tradition. It took her a day to get used to things but she observes, 'We have amazing bodies which just automatically can adapt to the surroundings. Never take your body for granted—keep it healthy.'

Once the shuttle has launched, the Mission Control Center takes over. More popular by its radio call sign—'Houston'—the Christopher C. Kraft Jr. Mission Control Center is the place from which the entire mission is monitored and managed. The Control Centre is constantly functional since there are always astronauts on the ISS. There are flight controllers, engineers who control the systems, the computer, the communication, the robotics, the duties and schedules, the PR activities . . . it's a busy,

busy place and the astronauts are regularly in touch with Mission Control during their space sojourn.

The ISS is quite like a ship so it's no surprise that nautical terms are used to describe it. For instance, the left and right sides are Port and Starboard, front and rear are Forward and Aft, top and bottom are Overhead and Deck. The first Commander to the ISS was Bill Shepherd, also a Navy man. He introduced one more naval tradition—the clanging of the bell. All new and visiting crew ring the bell that Shepherd hung in the ISS, as a sign announcing their arrival! He also coined the radio sign 'Alpha' for the ISS; when they call Mission Control, you'll hear the astronauts say—'Houston, this is Alpha calling . . .' There are several customs that are followed but that's another story for another day.

The ranking on the ISS

Commander—one who heads the mission. Must have been part of a prior space voyage/ expedition.

Mission Specialist—one who is assigned specific duties while aboard the ISS.

Pilot—has to assist the Commander, so has similar

qualifications as Commander but prior space experience is not necessary.
Flight Engineer—has the same duties as the Mission Specialist but must also be a trained pilot and be able to assist the Commander and the Pilot.
Science Officer—primarily responsible for the science experiments that are being conducted aboard the ISS.
Space Flight Participant—a tourist to the ISS, with no duties.

Hair-raising tales from space

The ISS itself orbits sixteen times—which makes for as many sunrises and sunsets. Pretty disorienting, don't you think? So to simplify matters, they use the Greenwich Mean Time to set their watches.

Within the first few days after arrival, Sunita had a rather unusual task on her to-do list—getting a haircut! After the naval academy, Sunita had begun to let her hair grow out again. When time came for her to go into space, she realized that in a microgravity environment, her hair would be a bit of a mess to manage—it would fly all over—upwards! But instead of cutting it off before the launch, she chose to fly with it, and just enjoy having her hair billowing about her before chopping it off. Her hair itself was sent back as a donation to Locks of Love, a charity that uses such donations to create prosthetics for children who lose hair due to illness.

'We kept an eye out for Santa!'

Sunita began maintaining a weekly journal narrating her experiences on the ISS, the cool places she saw, the food she ate and the workouts she never missed.

Sunita had arrived at the ISS on 11 December and she was scheduled to be here for six months. Soon it was time for Christmas. Sunita had missed Christmas at home before but it certainly was the first time she was so many miles away, looking out of the window at the whole planet, and imagining celebrations at home. But on the ISS itself, there was noise and bonhomie as well as Russian sugar cookies with Christmassy decorations. The Russian theme extended into their New Year celebration as well with a screening of a Russian movie called *Irony of Fate*. From the ISS, Sunita and the others watched the lights on Earth—the cities always shone brighter at night and on New Year's Eve, Sunita wrote, they saw fireworks over Naples!

The days soon took on a routine although every day was in some way unpredictable. One thing that could not be missed was her daily workout. In space, even within the ISS, there is little gravity, which means that astronauts soon start losing bone and muscle mass. Every month, the astronauts check their weight and measure their calves to make sure they are not losing too much weight. Usually the calves and around the ankles are where the muscle mass is first lost since no one walks. Which is why working out becomes crucial. Sunita started a workout plan for running/walking and cycling on alternate days along with daily weight training. All the equipment was engineered so that when an astronaut is running or jogging on them, the whole space station won't vibrate! That would indeed be a disaster. So the vibration is isolated to the machine. The treadmill is called TVIS or the Treadmill Vibration Isolation System the bike is CEVIS or Cycle Ergometer Vibration Isolation System, and the weight lifting device was RED or Resistive Exercise Device.

The ISS . . . continued

By the time Sunita was at the ISS, the station had the Russian module, Zarya (Sunrise), a US module,

Destiny, connecting the two was Unity, an airlock called the Quest, a docking area called Piers and a living segment called the Zvezda (Star). While the astronauts worked in their respective modules during the day, for meals and after-work lounging, they gathered at Zvezda.

Every morning, Sunita received her task list for the day. After breakfast, she would begin her duties. Besides the construction work on the ISS and the numerous scientific experiments, there was maintenance and cleaning as well. There are no electricians or plumbers, no mechanics to call to fix things. If the bike didn't function, the crew would get down to mending it, if the toilet broke down, the crew would try and patch it up. And of course, they had to make sure there was time to work out. Mealtimes, especially in the evening, were something they all looked forward to. Sunita's containers sometimes threw up some spicy Indian food like palak paneer and Punjabi chole and halva and she enjoyed them. They got to watch football games too—streamed by NASA. Their favourite entertainment shows were also streamed in and on weekends, the crew would put their feet up and catch up on TV.

Astronauts don't carry much luggage—they need a few clothes (very few since nothing gets dirty there), some personal items, but that's about it! There is no laundry on the ISS; the clothes are not washed and every time a new load arrives, the astronauts just get rid of the old ones. There is no kitchen on the ISS and nothing is cooked there; so food is sent up in a preserved form. Provisions rarely get exhausted since every few months, a supply vehicle is sent up to the ISS. These vehicles are all called *Progress* and carry food, equipment or material needed for experiments, clothes and so on. The *Progress* docks into the ISS and stays there until the next *Progress* is expected. At this time, all the trash is loaded on to the *Progress* before it is disconnected. When it undocks, the vehicle loses its ability to remain in orbit and is destroyed in space.

Into space

Work on the ISS construction continued and one of the things Sunita had to prepare for was the EVA or the spacewalk. The EVAs need a lot of preparation and among other things, the spacesuit has to be charged and readied for use. The tools have to be reviewed before the spacewalks are conducted because there is work to be done outside, sometimes experiments, sometimes repairs and everything must be planned and checked and rechecked several times. You can't just holler for a wrench or spanner from outside, you see. A big part of preparing for a spacewalk is something called 'pre-breathe'. In this process, all the nitrogen in the body has to be removed and this is done by breathing in higher concentrations of oxygen. Why is this done? When the astronaut steps out of the atmosphere of the ISS, gas bubbles can form in the body and cause severe pain in the joints—wrist, elbows, knees, shoulders . . . it's called 'the bends'. This happens also to deep-sea divers when the they hit the surface of the water on their way up. To avoid this, the astronauts get into their spacesuits several hours before they have to leave the station. The suit is filled with oxygen and for a few hours they breathe in this pure oxygen. This flushes the nitrogen out of the body and they are now ready to step out.

Sunita was up early to prepare for the EVA. By noon they were out of the airlock—Quest—through two doors, into space. For the next six to seven·hours, Sunita worked outside, tethered to the station. Astronauts also wear a SAFER or Simplified Aid for EVA Rescue. If an astronaut's tether comes loose and he or she starts to float away, this is used to return to the station. It's controlled with a joystick. EVAs are tiring because you work for such long hours without a break. There are no loo breaks either and astronauts have to wear a diaper.

While outside, Sunita got a great view of Patagonia of South America. She wrote, 'We really have the most beautiful planet in our solar system. None other can sustain life like we know it. None other has blue water and white clouds covering colourful land masses filled with thriving, beautiful, living things like human beings . . . I do hope there are other wonderful planets living and thriving out there, but ours is special because it is ours and ours to take care of. We really can't take that too lightly.'

Expedition 15

The arrival of the next set of cosmonauts marked the end of Expedition 14 and the commencement of Expedition 15. Cosmonauts Fyodor Yurchikhin and Oleg Kotov arrived on a Soyuz launch vehicle from Baikonur in Kazakhstan on 9 April 2007. With them too came

Charles Simonyi, a Hungarian-American who, believe it or not, was a space tourist! About two weeks later, Misha and LA returned to Earth on 21 April and Charles Simonyi returned with them on the Soyuz.

Sunita was scheduled to return on the SS *Atlantis* in April but ended up staying until 22 June. When it was time to leave, she knew she would miss being in space and on the ISS. Her farewell speech saw her choking back tears, 'I'm sad to say goodbye, but it's time for the International Space Station to grow a little more. You, the ISS, will always be a part of me, as you are a part of so many. You will pave the way for our future.' In her tribute to her fellow astronauts, ground crew, technicians and engineers, she said, 'These folks, along with their families, have dedicated their lives to ensure the success of astronauts and cosmonauts—along with exploration for the next generation.'

But it's the beginning of her speech that lingers . . . 'Exploration isn't necessary or logical. It is something that comes from inside each and every one of us. I believe we are all born with this curiosity for exploration. Human space flight is one aspect of it and it's one that I have been intimately familiar with for the past six months.'

Sunita's return was delayed by twenty-four hours due to bad weather on Earth. And with this one extra day, she broke the record for the longest single space flight by a woman. Sunita Williams had spent 195 days in space when she landed at the Edwards Air Force Base in California. And when she came out, Dina stood there, waiting with Sunita's beloved pet Gorby, the Jack Russell terrier, cradled in her arms.

Cool things Sunita did in space!

- RUN THE BOSTON MARATHON—Aboard the ISS, Sunita decided to 'run' the Boston Marathon (BM). While on Earth, she had run the Houston Marathon and qualified for the BM with a timing of three hours, twenty-nine minutes and fifty-seven seconds. 'I considered it a huge honour to qualify and I didn't want my qualification to expire without giving it a shot,' she said. The Boston Athletic Association sent her an official runner's bib—No. 14,000. Dina too decided to run the marathon on Earth. In Boston, 23,000 people began the race. It was raining heavily and the crowds pushed past each other to start. On the ISS, it was fairly quiet with most of the six-member crew still asleep. Sunita tethered herself to the treadmill TREAMIS and started running. Her goal was to complete 42.2 km. Minutes after she started, ground control joked, 'We estimate you've completed your marathon right now . . .' The ISS travels 7.7 km per second and in less than six minutes, it had covered that distance. Running on the TREAMIS puts a lot of strain on the legs and Sunita took several breaks to massage them, to adjust the harness and to drink water. The ground staff cheered her on, playing music and radioing updates about the race below. Oleg woke up and came over to cheer Sunita. He had brought oranges with him on the Soyuz and kept up a steady supply of fruit for Sunita. In four hours and twenty-four minutes, Sunita completed the marathon run. It was 6.23 GMT when she radioed her message to Ground Control—'I am done! Woo hoo!' She then celebrated with a post-race feast—curried vegetables with peanuts, chicken with peanut sauce!

- THREE SPACEWALKS WITHIN NINE DAYS—On 31 January 2007, Sunita and ISS Commander Mike Lopez-Alegria spent seven hours and fifty-five minutes outside the ISS to work on the power and cooling systems, part of the ISS construction. A second walk took place on 4 February and the third on the 8th. It was a record! Before Sunita's mission came to an end in April, she performed another EVA with the Expedition 15 team, making it the highest number of spacewalks by a woman. She reminiscences, 'We train so much for them that I didn't ever feel afraid. I felt like it was pretty natural to be out there first of all . . . When I had some free time, I looked up and saw us flying over our planet. I looked further up and saw the vastness of space with the millions of stars crystal clear above me. I saw the northern lights shimmering and dancing green above Earth's surface . . . From inside the station one can see some of this, but it was all there just in front of my vision.'

- **MEET THE QUEEN**—You heard right! One fine day the crew of Expedition 15 were asked to dress up a bit for the British monarch was visiting NASA's Goddard Space Flight Center in Maryland. While there, NASA was going to hook up to the ISS. Sunita, Oleg and Fyodor wore their official best and waited for the Queen who arrived dot on time.

The Queen got to see Suni's hair flying upwards, watched the microphone fly between the astronauts and listened to them describe their time on the ISS. Without a doubt, Her Majesty was fascinated with what she saw and heard.

- GROWING SOYBEANS—Several experiments are conducted on the ISS and one of them was to see how plants thrive in a microgravity environment. When the soybeans sprouted, Sunita wrote excitedly, 'I have my mother's green thumb.'
- BEING ON TELEVISION—Celebrity talk show hostess Martha Stewart interviewed Sunita and LA for her show. They showed her the soybean sprouts they were growing on the ISS and asked her for tips on making their meals more inviting. Sunita's sister Dina joined in from the audience.
- CALLING TIM SHANKS ON ALVIN—*Alvin* is a submersible, a vehicle used for underwater work and owned by the Woods Hole Oceanographic Institute, MA, where Dina works. Alvin was two miles below water with marine biologist Tim Shanks working on it. Sunita was 200 miles above on the ISS and the two had a conversation via a sea to space phone connection.

'Alpha calling Alvin,' announced Sunita. 'We are looking at the ocean hoping you're having a good time down there.' Both chatted about their jobs and a typical day at work before signing off.

- GETTING TRICKED INTO CLEANING THE LOO—The urine containers have to be emptied into the *Progress* as trash. Wrote Sunita, 'The conversation went something like this:

  Misha : They only let really experienced people do this.

  Sunita : What do you mean? I understand how this system works.

  Misha : I am not sure you really know enough.

  Sunita : I can learn, please teach me.

  Misha : Okay, but only if you promise not to tell anyone and don't screw it up!

  Sunita : Oh great! Thank you, thank you . . .

  Seven urine tanks later, I realized he had pulled a Tom Sawyer on me!'

- HAM RADIO PASSES—Most astronauts are licensed amateur radio operators and Sunita's call sign is KD5PLB. The HAM radio is one of the ways in which she regularly had chats with schoolchildren and science groups across Earth. ARISS as it's called—Amateur Radio on the ISS—is a big part of NASA's Education outreach. How it works is that when the ISS is passing over a city or town, an operator on Earth can pick up the signal and establish contact. There is usually only a ten-minute window but schools were generally made aware of the schedule in advance and would prepare their questions. Sunita spoke to several groups during her stay on the ISS.

- TALKING TO CESAR MILAN, THE DOG WHISPERER—Sunita missed Mike. She missed her parents and sister. She missed her friends. But more than everyone, she missed little Gorby, her Jack Russell terrier, who didn't know why he could hear Sunita but not see or smell her. So she was keen on the chat with Cesar Milan, popularly known as the Dog Whisperer and asked him questions on how to help young Gorby deal with her being away for so long. For Sunita, a dog lover, it was the highlight of the week.
- LOOKING OUT OF THE WINDOW—Sarah, a girl scout aged eleven, asked Sunita what she felt looking at Earth from space. Sunita replied, 'It makes me

smile! Different parts of the world have distinct characteristics. The US, of course, we know, so it brings familiar faces. South America, especially down south near the glaciers, looks very rugged and inviting. The land is chocolate brown. Europe is fun because we know what different land masses look like, Italy for example. The Middle East and the Sahara in Africa are pinkish from the vast sand. Wind erosion there is obvious. India and the Far East look mysterious to me because you can see there is a lot going on there. But really what I see is a very beautiful place, full of colour. There are no borders that are really obvious. It makes me feel like all of us are humans, no matter where we are from, what our backgrounds are, that we should be having fun together. I can't imagine even a person arguing down there, not to mention fighting. I love looking at our planet. It is beautiful!'

Space Tourists

He was not an astronaut. Nor was he a pilot or a scientist. He was not going to be on the ISS for very long either. What's more, he had paid for his ticket! His name was Charles Simonyi and he was a space tourist!

Simonyi, of Hungarian origin but currently American resident, is a software architect who became the fifth space tourist. How does one book a flight to space? Well, Space Adventures is the 'travel agency' for space tourists. Beginning in 2001, it has arranged for orbital space trips for people. Needless to say, it's a very, very expensive holiday but there have been quite a few who have been able to afford it. In fact, Charles Simonyi enjoyed his first trip so much that he went there a second time! A manned flight to the Moon is next on their agenda. Of his trip to space, Simonyi said, 'The view is indeed incredible and it always changes, just like on a cruise ship, but faster. When, for example, New York comes up, everybody drops everything and comes to the windows to ooh and aah. Fortunately we are somewhere else in twenty seconds otherwise nobody would get any work done!'

Meanwhile on Earth . . .

During Sunita's space sojourn, her family kept in touch with her through email and weekly video chats. Sunita missed them and Mike but she could see and talk to them. Who she missed much much more was Gorby. No story about Sunita can be complete without the story of Gorby. Sunita and Michael already had Turbo, a Labrador retriever when she brought the little terrier home in 2001. Sunita was by then spending time in Russia and decided to name the pup Gorby after the Soviet president Mikhail Gorbachev who is credited with bringing great democratic reforms to the USSR. Gorby soon became Sunita's constant companion; he was small enough to travel with her everywhere and so he did. When Sunita took off on the *Discovery*, Gorby was there to watch the launch. On the ISS, Sunita carried a little stuffed Gorby to keep her company. People began to recognize him from interviews and Sunita often spoke about missing him. On Earth, Gorby's pictures seemed to set off a Gorbymania and Sunita's colleagues at NASA put up pictures of Gorby at their offices and on their computers.

The picture of him was called Flat Gorby after a children's book character named Flat Stanley. When a team of astronauts went on their underwater NEEMO mission during Sunita's time on the ISS, NASA sent them a giant fridge magnet of Flat Gorby as the mascot.

For the time that Sunita was away on the ISS, Gorby went to live with her parents in Boston. The Pandya couple had moved from Needham to Falmouth once all the children had left home. Deepak continued to work and research at the university. Jay continued in the Navy for several years before leaving it to pursue a degree in Nuclear Technology. Dina meanwhile had finished college at Smith and went on to get an MBA from Babson College, also in Massachusetts. She joined the Woods Hole Oceanographic Institute in Woods Hole,

MA. Sunita's daily Gorby update came from her sister. Michael meanwhile had also left the Navy to train in law enforcement. As a Federal Officer he travelled across the country before settling for Houston as home.

Sunita's return to Earth was met with much relief and celebration. In India, there were prayers being offered for her safe return. The SS *Columbia* was still a raw wound for those who remembered and missed Kalpana.

All astronauts on their return take a little time to get their 'Earth legs' back. Returning astronauts have to get used to gravity once again. Those who have been on long missions must remember not to throw things and expect them to float rather than fall. It takes a few months for them to feel normal again. And along with their rehab, there are important debriefings where the astronauts have to discuss the work they did, the experiments they conducted and so on to the staff here. A big part of the astronaut's job post mission is public relations. Astronauts travel extensively to talk about the work on the ISS. And among Sunita's travels was a visit to India.

In September 2007, Sunita and her father arrived in India. It was Sunita's third trip to her father's home country. They landed in Ahmedabad where members of her extended family received her joyously. Sunita and Deepak visited Jhulasan. They were keen to visit Mahatma Gandhi's Sabarmati Ashram. It was one of the high points of their trip. Sunita spoke to students in Ahmedabad and Mumbai, and she met the then Indian president, Pratibha Patil. Sunita also flew to Hyderabad to speak at the International Astronautical Congress. It was a busy week that took her to places old and new. Sunita met the then Indian PM Manmohan Singh who called her an inspiration and a role model for women. The Prime Minister also announced the Sunita Williams Scholarships for Higher Education in Space.

Sunita returned home and continued her work at the Astronaut Office at the Johnson Space Center. Between February 2008 and October 2009 Sunita was the Deputy Chief of the Astronaut Office. And in this role, she would sometimes represent NASA at mission launches, assist astronauts by sharing her experiences and of course, do a lot of PR work. In the years that followed, awards and commendations came. ABC Television named her Person of the Week.

Colby College conferred on her an honorary doctorate. She received the Navy Commendation Medal. The World Gujarati Society awarded her with the Sardar Vallabhbhai Patel Vishwa Pratibha Award, making her the first non-Indian citizen to receive it. The Indian government conferred the Padma Bhushan on her. Sunita Williams was now a celebrity. In her trademark NASA uniform, speaking at events across the world, Sunita became a familiar sight and the only thing that changed was the length of her hair; she had started to grow it out once more.

The construction of the ISS had continued through the years and in 2010, the construction was complete—the ISS now was a fully functioning laboratory orbiting Earth and expected to orbit for several years. Several long missions had continued and Sunita began training as back up crew for Expedition 30 that was scheduled for 2011. (All expeditions have back up crews in case an astronaut is unable to go.) Sunita herself was selected to take part in Expeditions 33 and 34. So really, it was back to school in Russia and some really intensive preparation schedules. There were a lot of changes since Sunita's first space sojourn.

The International Space Station was huge! As long as a football field and with giant solar panels forming its wings, weighing over 4,00,000 kgs, the ISS was now a fully functional lab with US, Russian, European and Japanese modules. Each expedition now included six astronauts where earlier there had been only three. Also by now, the US had no space shuttles that were being used to launch astronauts. The pride of the American space programme had been its five space shuttles, *Challenger*, *Columbia, Discovery, Endeavour* and *Atlantis.* In 1986, the *Challenger* met with the first big accident, killing all seven of the crew—six astronauts and one Teacher in Space Participant, Christa McAuliffe. The shuttle disintegrated within seconds after the launch. SS *Columbia* disintegrated with seven astronauts including Kalpana Chawla in 2003. In 2011, the *Atlantis* was retired and in 2012, the *Discovery* was placed into its new home at the Smithsonian Natural History Museum. A few months later, SS *Endeavour* went on its last flight, marking the end of an era for the American space programme. With this move, all launches to the ISS were shifted to Baikonur with the Soyuz as the launch vehicle.

The Soyuz is quite different from the space shuttle; while the shuttle could carry up to seven astronauts, on the Soyuz, only three can go and it is a little more cramped inside. But it is far more reliable than the Shuttle and in the recent years has not caused any fatalities. Also, where the space shuttle could double up as a lab, the Soyuz is strictly a delivery vehicle.

Onwards and upwards—first stop, Baikonur. Next stop, space

Sunita's launch was scheduled for 15 July 2012 at 8.40 a.m. Baikonur time. Sunita was to travel with Aki Hoshida of the Japanese Aeronautical Agency and cosmonaut Yuri Malchenko on Expeditions 33 and 34. In June, Bonnie visited Sunita for a week. Mike and Dina too were expected for the launch. With two weeks to go before the launch, Sunita, Aki and Yuri entered the last phase of their preparation. They shifted from Star City to Baikonur, to the Cosmonaut Hotel. There were exams to pass followed by a week-long quarantine. And of course, the haircut.

Sunita flies on the Soyuz!

Sunita enjoyed her Soyuz ride. On her blog, Sunita wrote, 'There is water, food and a toilet. The food is all

Russian: cans of meat and fish, cheese, cookies and juice in little juice boxes. It was like camping. We slept a lot, ate our food and used the toilet. Of course we chatted and laughed. Luckily Dina brought me a Sudoku book, so I ripped out a couple pages, put them in my flight books and did a couple of puzzles in my free time.' Once more the launch took all of eight minutes but it was two days before they would dock at the ISS.

Some Strange, Some Not so Much—Traditions before the Soyuz Launch!

Two weeks before launch—All astronauts prepare to leave Star City for Baikonur. But first, they stop at Gagarin's memorial on Cosmonauts' Memorial and lay red carnations there. Gagarin died in a plane crash in 1968 and this important tradition is a tribute to the first man in space. The astronauts also sign the Visitors Book at the Gagarin Museum. Arriving in Baikonur, they check into the Cosmonaut Hotel. All astronauts also plant a sapling. The Cosmonaut Avenue in Baikonur is lined with trees, each of which has been planted by an astronaut who has flown from here.

Five days before launch—Flag-raising ceremony where the

astronauts raise their country's flag, and also the Kazakh flag. Signing of books and memorabilia follows.

Two days before launch—The rocket is rolled out. The crew are not allowed to view it as it is considered bad luck. Instead, they get their hair trimmed or cut.

The night before launch—Viewing of the Russian film, *White Sun of the Desert!*

Day of the launch—Raise a toast, sign the doors of their hotel room, sit down for a few seconds before moving forward. A Russian Orthodox priest blesses the crew before they leave. The buses that take the astronauts to the launch pad have two horseshoes for luck. It's a forty-minute ride to the site of the launch and the bus stops for another tradition—the male astronauts will take a leak on the bus tyres (a practice that began with Yuri Gagarin and has since been jokingly referred to as 'anointing the bus tyres').

By the way, the date 24 October is never chosen for a launch—in 1960 the R-16 rocket prototype exploded killing seventy-four people and again in 1963 on the same date, an R-9 rocket caused a fire causing the death of seven people.

The Home Office

Already on the ISS were Sergei Revin, Gennady Padalka and Joe Acaba. With the arrival of Sunita, Aki and Yuri, the six-member Expedition 32 was all set with Gennaldy as the Commander. The ISS was bigger than it was when Sunita had last visited. It now had a living room, a kitchen, a bathroom, bedroom, toilet, closet and offices and even a home gym! Of course, these spaces don't look like they do on Earth—the 'bedroom' was actually sleeping stations on the walls, floor and ceiling where each station had a sleeping bag and space for a computer and some personal things; the living room was one of the modules where everyone gathered for breakfast or dinner; you couldn't, of course, cook in the kitchen, but packets of dehydrated or frozen foods were stored here along with bonus containers that came with the supply vehicles and carried the astronauts' individual favourites; the toilets somewhat resembled the ones on Earth except . . . there was a tube for urine and a potty. The urine is passed through filters and recycled for water while the toilet waste becomes trash. Every two months or so when a supplies vehicle returns to Earth, the trash is loaded into it and much of it burns when the vehicle re-enters the atmosphere.

The 'offices' are the most exciting places—here's where the work that the space station has been built for is done. But perhaps everyone's favourite spot is the window seat—the Cuppola which is an observatory with seven windows, offering the best view of Earth, space and even of the ISS. When Sunita arrived here in 2012, the ISS weighed almost a million pounds, stood at as long as a football field at 357 feet, with an acre of solar panels that powered it, a fifty-five-feet long giant robotic arm that could lift upto 220 pounds, eight solar arrays . . . besides Zarya, Zvezda, Destiny, Unity and Quest there was also Columbus, the European lab, Kibo belonging to Japan, the Cuppola, Rassvelt, which is a mini research module, and a storage module called Leonardo.

Perhaps more than anything else, meals make a big difference to life on the ISS. Says Sunita, 'Food could potentially be one of those expedition-triggering issues—something that gets people mad at each other—so being semi-conscious of all this is important.' So over the years the kinds of food, the menu and the choices have evolved greatly. Each container of food is used within nine days. About nine containers are opened at a time and they offer an entire range of beverages, eggs, fruit, meats, sides, snacks, breads etc. There will inevitably be food that one likes a lot and also which one dislikes. How do the astronut choose? They begin by eating their most favourite food first and the next best and so on. Sunita advises, 'You never save something, because the other guys will then eat it and then you will be mad. So, just eat what you like, they eat what they like and then we end up eating the yucky stuff at the end. It works!'

The day on the ISS begins by 6 a.m. with music streaming on the PA system—everyday it's a different song. By 8 p.m. they are done for the day and by 10, it's lights out! Weekends are for cleaning, maintenance and of course, catching up with family and friends back home. Sometimes even a movie or game is thrown in.

Getting ready for the races

Almost immediately after her arrival on the ISS Sunita began exercising. The trusty old CEVIS was still going strong and there was a new machine—the ARED or the Advanced Resistive Exercise Device, which soon became Sunita's favourite exercise equipment. The ARED is a bit of a design marvel; it provides weights and resistance allowing for the kind of workout that is crucial in the microgravity environment. Because there is almost no gravity, the body doesn't need the skeleton to hold it up and the calcium from the bones starts getting redistributed. Consequently muscle also begins to break down. To combat this, astronauts need to work out a couple of hours everyday or risk losing too much bone density and muscle mass—which means that when they return they will feel like a much, much older person.

The Olympics were on around that time and in the 'evenings' all six crew members would get together to watch the live streaming videos of the Games from NASA. With the Games ongoing on Earth, Sunita planned her races in space. The first one coming up was the 7.2 mile Falmouth Road Race. Dina and several of their friends were taking part. Sunita decided to join in too. The night before the race, she video chatted with her parents, her sister and some of the runners. Sunita's number was emailed to her and she printed it out. The next morning, she waited on the TREMIS for the race to commence. Sunita was on time. But the race didn't begin. It was raining in Falmouth! Ten minutes later, the race opened and Sunita started running. She completed it in one hour, three minutes and fifty-two seconds.

The next race was scheduled in September, the Nautica Malibu Triathlon. This was harder than the marathon she had run. First there was a .8 km swim that Sunita did on the ARED, followed by 29 kms on the CEVIS and a 6.4 km run on the TREAMIS. It took Sunita one hour, forty-eight minutes and thirty-three seconds. 'It wasn't easy,' she admitted. 'I'm happy to be done.'

Stepping out for a spacewalk

On this mission too, Sunita had to plan for the EVA or Extra Vehicular Activity as the spacewalk is called. Preparations for it began in early August itself. The EVA was scheduled for Sunita and Aki for the 30th. The spacesuits had to be taken out and checked thoroughly.

Batteries had to be charged, the tools all gathered and readied. They had to review the tasks they would do outside, discussing emergency procedures—what if they lose communication with mission control, what if something goes wrong with the suit, what if the tasks take longer than planned, what if . . . As Sunita says, 'Even planning when to go to sleep and what to eat are important. Remember, you are in that suit usually about eight hours for a six hour EVA . . .' Sunita had a pre-EVA tradition of her own—she ate Fluffernutters—wheat bread sandwiches with peanut butter and her favourite marshmallow cream, Fluff, and Tvoreg, a Russian delicacy that Sunita describes as a cross between cottage cheese and cream cheese with nuts.

On the spacewalk, Sunita and Aki had to install a Main Bus Switching Unit and a camera on the robotic arm. But they came up against a 'sticky bolt'. So after ten hours outside, Sunita and Aki returned to plan for another EVA. The second EVA took place the same week and Sunita and Aki fixed the Main Bus Switching Unit, which provided a portion of the power to the ISS, and also fixed the camera on to the robotic arm. Their tasks done, it meant the EVAs were successful! The prolonged

EVAs outside also meant that Sunita had now logged the highest number of hours outside the ISS for a woman—a total of fifty hours and forty minutes, a record previously held by Peggy Whitson. From Earth, Peggy passed on her congratulations to Sunita, 'You go, girl!'

Science aboard the ISS

Sunita's work on the ISS this time included various scientific experiments. As Expedition 32 crew, they performed 201 investigations including blood cell testing, extreme weather observation, analyses of human hair exposed to a long-duration space flight . . . diverse experiments from biology to geography to physiology . . . This continued into Expedition 33 when blood, urine and saliva samples were analysed and tested which meant Sunita was regularly collecting samples to send to Earth. Earth Observations was another NASA-led experiment, and they photographed changes on the surface, floods, fires, volcanoes . . . When Sunita observed Hurricane Sandy over the north-eastern coast of the USA, she wrote, 'Hurricane Sandy and the Frankenstorm are covering up everything from the Chicago area to past the east coast from our vantage point. Now we can see the swirls . . . I hope Dad has Gorby tied down so he doesn't blow away . . .'

Sunita also received a biological payload of two spiders and several fruit flies (for the spiders!). YouTube Space Lab was a science contest held in 2011–12 when children were invited to submit microgravity experiments. There were two winners—Sara Ma and Dorothy Chen from Troy, Michigan won in the 14–16 year old category. Their experiment was on the theme 'Could Alien Superbugs Cure Disease on Earth?' And for this they sent up Bacillus subtilis to observe if the strain of bacteria growing in a microgravity environment is more infectious that what grows on Earth. The winner of the 17–18 category was Amr Mohammed from Egypt whose experiment was titled 'Can You teach an Old Spider New Tricks?' For this two zebra spiders—named Cleopatra and Nefertiti—were sent up to the ISS along with fruit flies. The experiment was to see if weightlessness will interfere with their ability to jump on their prey and if the spiders adapt to the new environment. The spiders spent a hundred days on the USS and the experiment showed that they had indeed adapted to the new environment. When it was time for their journey back home, it was a concerned and emotional Sunita who packed them for their return trip, bubble wrapping their habits and giving the boxes a hug before placing them in the Dragon SPACEX capsule. She wrote, 'I hope they make it. Little Cleo is being elusive again. Big dark Titi is in the corner . . . not moving much. I will be happy to pack them up—hopefully it isn't like I am putting them in a coffin . . . hang in there, there are many fruit flies on Earth . . . and no, we don't have bugs up here to my knowledge. Maybe bedbugs, but nothing floating/flying around in the open so releasing them here wouldn't be a good idea . . .' Sunita worried for the spiders, trying not to get too attached to them and not sure if they would make it back to Earth. Cleo died on touchdown but Nefertiti survived. She was taken to the Smithsonian Museum and was put on display. Here, however, she died four days later.

But there were also other, more cheerful experiments. One of Sunita's favourite investigative projects was the Meteron where she remotely drove a robot that was in Germany. Mars missions use robots and this experiment was to observe how an astronaut could control a robot from a spacecraft orbiting the planet. It's a less expensive and much safer option than sending an astronaut into unknown dangers. The robot on land was Lego Mindstorm and Sunita successfully manoeuvred it to perform its task, 'I didn't hit anything!' She was thrilled to report.

The days went by in working on the experiments, running maintenance tasks on the ISS and of course, Public Relations events. On weekends, the crew normally got time off to catch up with their families. 'Dina was in charge of running the show here on Earth,' says Deepak. 'We would get a communication from NASA about the date and time that we could conference with Sunita and Dina would arrange it. She would invite friends and we would gather in the living room and wait for Sunita to come on the polycom.' Several of their friends got to speak to Sunita, including one of her favourite teachers, Ms DiNapoli, from her middle school.

Holidays and parties

On this trip Sunita got to celebrate both her birthday and Gorby's! His came first on 13 September followed by Sunita's on the 19th. The crew had a party on Gorby's birthday. Some digging around in the service module unearthed dates, oysters, chocolate-covered espresso beans and chocolate pudding cake that made up a great party spread. Sunita's stuffed Gorby was brought out and everyone had a blast.

Sunita enjoyed celebrating her birthday aboard the ISS too. 'I can't think of a better place to spend a birthday,' she wrote. 'It was a great day—no, not a day off—but a great day to take a couple of minutes, look out of the window, check out our awesome planet which is home to so many species that couldn't live anywhere else, and think about all the cake and ice cream I have had in the past, on this day. It makes me smile just thinking about it!' At this time, only Aki and Yuri were on board with her. Gennady, Joe and Sergei had already returned. Sunita's birthday, 19 September is also Annual Pirate Day and Aki, Yuri and Sunita dressed up as pirates—with bandannas and eyepatches. They had a quite a party when Sunita tuned in to talk to her family on Earth. Dina and her parents had a cake for her and Sunita virtually blew the candles. The bonus containers came out at dinner with a feast of lobster, saag paneer, and yakatori, a Japanese dish of skewered bacon or pork in sauce and good luck Japanese rice with red beans.

The Indian tricolour was hung up on the ISS on two special days—15 August, India's Independence Day and on Diwali. She thanked everyone for their prayers and support.

Catching up on the ISS

If you ever wondered whether life gets boring on the ISS, think again. With all the activity and with the Cuppola for the best view of Earth, there is little time to mope and sulk. And even when Sunita, Aki and Yuri were the only ones on board between the two crews that joined them, they found enough to keep them going. Wrote Sunita, 'I went down to the Russian end of the station to just ask Yuri a question, and I found myself there for over an hour and a half. We just had so much to talk about, the next couple weeks of activities, exercise philosophies, the new crew, the landing process, our families, rumours at home, the news, the origin of names, etc. We had each other cracking up . . . I did find Aki a little later in a remote part of the Japanese segment, practising his ukulele!'

Things you need to learn and unlearn in space

- FLOATING—it takes a couple of days to get used to floating without knocking into things. Flying around is not so much like Harry Potter—'I feel a little more like Mary Poppins without the umbrella. Remember when she landed at their house? Everyday is like that for me . . .' records Sunita.
- BRUSHING TEETH, BATHING, WASHING HAIR—there is no running water and since one doesn't get dirty in space, the astronauts just sponge themselves off. But they do sweat a lot up there and sweat clings to the skin in globules so regular wiping down is necessary. Washing hair with a little water and shampoo is a bit more challenging though.
- USING THE TOILET—there is a urine hose and a potty and aiming is crucial or else there will be a lot of cleaning up to do! During an EVA and during the launch, they use diapers.
- SLEEPING—the astronauts don't sit down and when they lie down in their sleeping bags, there is never a sense of being in bed. Usually they just strap themselves down to remain in position. And they are never 'lying

down'. In the absence of gravity, there is no direction so from another angle, they could be 'standing up'.

- CRYING—it's hard to enjoy a good cry in space. Tears just bubble up and get bigger and spread over your face until you wipe them!
- WARDROBE—you get used to a limited wardrobe. Usually astronauts get a pair of shorts and tee shirt for every three days of exercising. They remain in their work wear—shirt and pants/shorts—which is changed every ten days. Underwear and socks are changed every other day. They also get two sweaters. The shoes they wear for the treadmill are different from the ones that are used for the cycle. When the clothes are used as much as they can, they are disposed off in the *Progress* supply vehicle and they burn on re-entry along with the trash.
- EATING—if you toss a peanut up, it won't land in your mouth! If you open a tube of Wasabi paste, like Sunita once did, it will fly everywhere and take weeks to clean. If you enjoy cooking the ISS is not the place to unwind by whipping up something yummy. Most of the food needs to be rehydrated before they can be eaten but sometimes fruit, desserts and even ice cream have made their way to the astronauts.

Spot the Station

The ISS isn't too far away from Earth, only about 400 kms. And it's so big that it's visible to the naked eye. You can actually see the ISS in the sky. Just register on NASA's Spot the Station updates here—spotthestation.nasa.gov—and you'll get a mail informing you of the time and date when the ISS will be clearly visible at your location. If you see it at night, it appears like a star—bright but unlike a star it doesn't flicker and it moves really fast so there's no missing it.

8

Safe Landings

On 19 November, 125 days after her launch, Sunita, Aki and Yuri suited up, floated over to the Soyuz that was docked at the ISS, made sure that that hatches were all shut properly, undocked and began their return.

The Soyuz has three parts—an orbital module, a descent module and a propulsion module. The astronauts sit in the descent module where they are strapped to their seats. The orbital and propulsion modules are detached from the capsule to burn when they re-enter the atmosphere. When the capsule reaches the atmosphere, the exterior starts heating up. It's also plummeting towards Earth at a very high speed. So, within the module are controls for the astronauts to navigate. The rate of descent is decreased gradually and four parachutes are deployed fifteen minutes before landing. Of these, the largest chute is the most visible as it carries the astronauts to Earth. The seats inside are lined with shock absorbers to cushion the landing but it's a bit of a bumpy ride all the same. Inside the module, the astronauts become aware of their homecoming when their arms no longer float, the head seems to weigh a ton and standing up is near impossible. It's an unmistakable return to gravity.

When Sunita and her crew landed, they remained in their seats. They knew they were in Kazakhstan but with a parachute landing, the Search and Rescue Team takes a while to reach the spot—they wait in their helicopters at a distance to also avoid the blades interfering with the parachutes. Twenty minutes later, the Search and Rescue team had reached the capsule and the three astronauts were helped out. It was the middle of a winter night and despite the cold, there was jubilation at their safe return.

Sunita, Aki and Yuri were taken to Baikonur and then on to Russia. A long flight later, Sunita was in Houston. Her parents and Dina had flown down with Gorby. Sunita stepped out of the plane to meet her family, just a little unsteady on her Earth legs.

This time, too, Sunita couldn't help but miss the ISS intensely. Four months had just flown by. She said, 'It was a sad day for us, a little bittersweet, when we got back.' She missed the ISS but returning home she did the one thing that she couldn't do in space—dial a pizza!

It takes weeks to months for astronauts to recover from living in a microgravity environment. They have several physical checks where they are monitored, besides debriefing meetings where they discuss the work done on the ISS. Both of her space missions were followed by several public relations activities. Almost six months were devoted to PR-related activities. And thanks to her parents, both India and Slovenia threw her big welcoming parties after both missions. And as one who connects equally to the two countries, Sunita had enjoyed both samosas and Slovenian sausages on the ISS!

In March 2013, Sunita arrived in India once more. And yet again, there were large crowds of people eager to meet her and hear about her experiences. Many young people asked her how they too could become astronauts. Several wanted to know what it was like to float in space. Again and again, Sunita enthusiastically shared her stories. A trip to Slovenia followed where Sunita met relatives from her mother's side of the family. The Slovenian president conferred a decoration on her for her contribution to the promotion of natural sciences and for being a role model for young Slovenians.

But Sunita Williams, like Kalpana Chawla before her, stresses on the lack of borders. Sunita is a great believer in the unifying nature of the space programme. There has been enormous trust displayed in the building of the space station and bringing people from different countries together for a common goal. Says Sunita, 'I think it is a role model programme for many, many other international programmes on the ground . . . My own personal feeling is that when you leave the planet, you sort of leave as a human being. You are citizens of Earth.'

The PR work is exhausting and for about six months after her return Sunita travelled extensively. Besides India and Slovenia, she went to several places within the United States, visiting several schools, including those in Needham and Falmouth—her home. Her father, who accompanied her on some of these trips, was amazed at the energy and enthusiasm she displayed, untiringly answering questions from people—both children and adults. Sunita finds these interactions almost more exhausting than space flights but thinks it's a great opportunity to communicate with people and share with them her experiences as an astronaut.

A little reflection

Every single launch and return carries a certain amount of risk and while all attempts are made to minimize it, a safe journey and a safe return are always much to be thankful for. Sunita's first space mission was on the heels of the SS *Columbia* accident and friends and family were understandably nervous as she prepared to come back to Earth. In Kalpana's village in Haryana, school children prayed for Sunita's safe return. In Ahmedabad, Deepak's home town, priests performed rituals to ensure the same. Everyone breathed a sigh of enormous relief when the shuttle landed safely and Sunita stepped out of it.

The second mission was perhaps a little less stressful for the Soyuz is known to be reliable. But nevertheless every mission has uncertainties that accompany it. In a recent interview, Sunita spoke candidly, 'You also have to prepare yourself. I call it tying up the ends of your life before you go because you never know what's going to happen. You want to make sure that when you leave, you feel at peace with everything . . .'

Not all days spent in space are easy—one misses family and friends and although astronauts can make phone calls or communicate with people back home, they must find something to keep going. For Sunita, it was always the view of Earth from the Cuppola that made her smile.

Looking ahead . . .

Sunita was deployed in Russia for a year, heading the US segment at Star City as Director of Operations. Her experiences are of immense value for astronauts to learn from and that was a big part of her work for the year, along with working on Soyuz launches.

Sunita's father travelled to Russia and Star City for the first time in October. Sunita made sure the visit would include a trip to Leo Tolstoy's home in Yasnaya Polyana. Sunita's mother travelled to Russia in February and in between Gorby too got to spend time with her.

One year later, it was time for Sunita to return home to Houston and she chose the long way back on the Trans-Siberian Railways to Vladivostok. Arriving back in the US in summer, she says, is always a good thing to transition between two different kinds of lives, two different countries.

'The ISS has been my life since I joined NASA,' she says, remembering her first year when she viewed the beginnings of the ISS construction. I can recall every flight that's gone up to the ISS. And so she continues working at the Johnson Space Center involved with a host of activities such as astronaut selection and trainings and future Soyuz launches. And she has to keep up with her swimming and running and, of course, her flying.

The future looks exciting—perhaps another mission, perhaps even one to Mars. There's work on Mission Mars that has been ongoing, and the *Orion* is being hailed as the next gen space vehicle with capabilities to fly beyond the low Earth orbit, to carry crew, function as a lab and provide for a safe return. The possibilities are endless. But through all this, an older lingering dream has resurfaced in Sunita: that of becoming a middle-school science teacher. She finds herself increasingly thinking about it and perhaps that's where her path ahead lies. It sounds like a more sedate plan compared to space missions but if the past is anything to go by, it might mark the beginning of yet another adventure for Sunita Williams.

Do You Want To Be an Astronaut?

So if you want to become an astronaut, it is important to pursue a foundation in the sciences and to remain physically fit. You must be comfortable with remaining in confined spaces for long periods and of course, do gear up for long years of training. Teamwork and leadership skills are essential.

In India, there is a lot of interest in space and aeronautics. The Indian Space Research Organization (ISRO) has several ongoing space programmes. Science missions have been planned and a human space flight is also in the works. The Indian astronauts will be called 'vyomanauts'. They will be selected from among fighter pilots of the Indian Air Force. An Astroanut Training Centre will be established in Bangalore and the ISRO will launch the vyomanauts in its own vehicle, the GSLV-Mk III. Although originally scheduled for 2015, there have been delays. But do keep an eye out for more news.

TRIVIA TREASURY

Sunita Williams—A Timeline

1965: Born on 19 September in Euclid, Ohio

1983: Graduated from Needham High School

1987: Graduated from the US Naval Academy as ensign

1987–1993: Joined Navy Air, completed aviator training and was assigned to Helicopter Combat Support Squadron 8 at Virginia

1993: Year-long programme at the Naval Test Pilot School, Maryland

1993: Applied first time to NASA. Application rejected

1995: Completed Master's degree in Engineering Management from the Florida Institute of Technology

1997: Applied second time to NASA. Got the call from Astronaut Office in 1998

1998: Moved to Houston to work at NASA. Began astronaut training

2002: Selected for a space mission

2003: SS *Columbia* crashed killing all seven astronauts on board including Kalpana Chawla. The next few missions are cancelled.

2005: Space missions resumed

9 December 2006: Sunita's first space mission, eight years after joining NASA

23 June 2007: Sunita returned to Earth, spent 195 days in space, longest single space flight by a woman at that time.

15 July 2012: Sunita's second launch from Baikonur on a Soyuz

19 November 2012: Sunita returned to Earth, after 125 days on the ISS.

Women in Space

It was Soviet cosmonaut Valentina Tereshkova who was the first woman to go to space in 1963. She flew on the *Vostok* capsule which, on return, could not land safely. Valentina ejected with a capsule at some 7000 feet and landed unhurt. For about ten years after Valentina's successful space sojourn, there were surprisingly no women astronauts until Svetlana Savitskaya went up in

1982. Svetlana also holds the record for being the first woman to walk in space and also the first to go on two space flights. The US sent Sally Ride into space in 1983. She was only thirty-two years old, the youngest American astronaut so far. The first Teacher in Space was Barbara Morgan, who taught science at an elementary school in Idaho. Anna Lee Fisher was the first mother in space when she went on a mission in 1984 for seven days. In the last fifty years since Valentina Tereshkova flew to space, there have been fifty-seven (as of 2013) women artronauts from the United States, Russia, Canada, Korea, Japan, France, India, Iran and China.

Space Junk

Ever since space exploration began and man has been sending satellites there has been a major problem—space debris that has been accumulating over the years. The stages of the rocket that are jettisoned, satellites that are now defunct, fragments caused from collisions, from disintegration and even erosion . . . all of these continue to orbit our planet. It's a big cause for worry because the junk can hit and damage the ISS and other satellites leading to very severe consequences. According to NASA's Orbital Debris Office, 'More than 21,000 orbital debris larger than 10 cm are known to exist. The estimated population of particles between 1 and 10 cm in diameter is approximately 5,00,000. The number of particles smaller than 1 cm exceeds 100 million.' Most of these are within 2000 km of the atmosphere—the low Earth orbit.

This debris is moving at a rapid rate of 7–8 km per second. The higher the altitude, the longer they remain in orbit before eventually entering the atmosphere when they will plummet towards the earth and either burn or fall. But this may take from decades to centuries depending on how high they are.

Mars Rovers

Several vehicles have been sent to Mars and among them are the rovers—automated motor vehicles that actually explore the planet and beam back images. The Sojurner was a miniature rover that landed in Mars in 1997 and explored the red planet for about three months. Spirit was next, landing in Mars in Jan 2004 and joined three weeks later by its twin, Opportunity. Spirit worked until 2010 when its communication with Earth ended.

Scientists believe the extreme Martian winter may have rendered several critical parts damaged. Opportunity is still going strong and has been joined by Curiosity, launched in November 2011. Mars exploration goals are to determine whether life existed on Mars, characterize the climate and geology of the planet and to help prepare for human exploration of it.

Lunar Landings

Like the Mars rovers, a few were sent to the Moon also—the Lunakhod 1 and 2 from the USSR were the 'moon walkers'. While Lunakhod 1 lasted over thirty years, Lunakhod 2 is still there. The US Apollo missions sent up the Apollo Lunar Roving Vehicle during the early seventies. India sent up the *Chandrayan 1* in 2008 which was operational for 312 days. It was intended to remain there for two years but technical glitches didn't permit that. However, *Chandrayan* did much for India's space programme and has been credited with the discovery of water molecules on lunar soil. *Chandrayan 2* is already in the pipeline while NASA is working on ATHLETE (All Terrain Hex-Legged Extra Terrestrial Explorer) and Scarab.

Books on Astronauts and Space Flights (some wildly imaginative ones)

George's Secret Key to the Universe (Doubleday 2007), *George's Cosmic Treasure Hunt* (Simon & Schuster, 2009) and *George and the Big Bang* (Simon & Schuster, 2011) by Lucy and Stephen Hawking: A great combination of fact and fiction by the father-daughter duo. (Fiction/Non-fiction)

The Story of Astronomy and Space by Louie Stowell and Peter Allen (Usborne, 2009): An unintimidating introduction to space, stars, planets and all things astronomy. (Non-fiction)

Neil Armstrong–Young Pilot (Aladdin, 1996); *John Glenn—Young Astronaut* (Aladdin, 2000). Both titles in the *Childhood of Famous Americans* series. This is a great introduction to two pioneering astronauts in a very readable and engrossing format. (Biography)

Space Race by Tom Clohosy Cole (Nobrow Press, 2012): An illustrated chronicle of the space era. It's a beautifully visual book and if you can find it, you must add to your collection! (Illustrated)

Astronaut Academy (Macmillan, 2011): A series of manga comics with the first one out, called *Zero Gravity*. Set in a middle school in outer space, it seems to be quickly gathering a fan following. (Fiction)

Cosmic by Frank Cottrell Boyce (Macmillan, 2009): The story of Liam, an extremely tall boy who mistakenly finds himself on an 'out-of the world' adventure. (Fiction)

Larklight by Philip Reeve (Bloomsbury, 2007): Art and his sister Myrtle live in a huge house, Larklight, with their father. The house incidentally is orbiting in space, way beyond the Moon. One day, they are informed about an impending visitor, which is a rather unusual occurence. Their guest sets off mysterious happenings and Art and his family are now battling to save the universe.